*Ecstasy
is the higher self
in action.*

ECSTASY
IS A NEW FREQUENCY

◇ CHRIS GRISCOM ◇

Teachings of The Light Institute

with an introduction by
BARBARA HAND CLOW

BEAR & COMPANY
SANTA FE, NEW MEXICO

Dedicated to my higher self.

Library of Congress Cataloging-in-Publication Data

Griscom, Chris, 1942–
    Ecstasy is a new frequency.

    1. Light Institute (Galisteo, NM)   2. Griscom, Chris,
    1942–   3. Spiritual healing.   4. New Age movement.
I. Title
BP605.L53G75 1987   299'.93   87-11376
ISBN 0-939680-41-6

Bear & Company
P.O. Drawer 2860
Santa Fe, NM 87504

Design & Illustration: Angela C. Werneke
Cover Photography: Herbert Lotz
Typography: Casa Sin Nombre, Ltd.
Printed in the United States of America by BookCrafters

CONTENTS

ACKNOWLEDGMENTS

I profoundly thank Barbara and Gerry Clow who truly went beyond the laws of manifestation to produce this book! To Sue Kurman for accepting the Herculean challenge of typing the manuscript. Thank you, Angela Werneke, your creative gifts as designer are greatly appreciated. To Jim Young and all Bear & Company staffers who have lent your energies to bringing this book forward.

I deeply honor and thank my beloved colleagues who tirelessly bring these teachings to the world: Barbara Gluck, Karin Griscom, Susan Harris, Paula Kaufman, Richard Noll, and Rick Phillips. To Richard Benjamin and David Griscom whose beautiful cranial work is so vital to The Light Institute process. To Connie Dillon and Gay Lynn Olsen at The Light Institute whose love for this work inspires us all. To Joyce DeWitt, Shaina Noll, and Helen Soos who so lovingly upheld this vision all the way through. To Tuss Callanan, whose advice and creative wisdom has been of great help to me. To everyone who has ever laid upon my table—YOU are the source and inspiration of this book!

To my children/teachers: Karin, David, Britt, Megan, Teo, and Bapu. Thank you! And to you, too—Dakota Rafael. Special thanks to Julie and Serapio Anaya, Sandy Danziger and Patty Taylor.

INTRODUCTION

In each generation, there are a few books which say something new. *Ecstasy is a New Frequency* is one of those books. Chris Griscom offers us a key survival tool that we require at this time: her teaching on clearing the emotional body. Time is not circular, time is spiraling, and at certain special times like ours there is a build-up of energy, of consciousness, when we can "jump the spiral." All we have to do is choose to take the leap. Experience does not need to be an endless round of emergences from the underworld or an endless series of incarnations on the Wheel of Karma; we can jump the spiral and choose to become citizens of the galaxy, of the universe.

We were created to experience the story of the cosmos, to live the dream of creation, to tell the story of life within the matrix of animals, plants, and minerals. But, right now, we have lost our way because of the accumulation of thousands of years of lifetimes which exist within us as impacted fear and guilt. All of these lives are inner voices crying out for release, because the time to open the doors of the prison within is now. But the accumulation of all the history, all the pain and fear of separation, is like a deafening roar of monsters within. So, we live our lives as an endless routine of material and emotional distraction, trying not to hear our inner screaming. We are finding we cannot quiet the inner fear. We all know we are getting sick from the polluted environment, which is a reflection of our inner illness. There is not a single one of us who does not anxiously observe the struggle of children to survive in our increasingly hostile ecosystem. Most of us know that the rising tide of Alzheimer's disease and cancer is a warning about the future for all. Some of us also sense that we are at the darkest point in an old cycle, and we can see many signs of new life and energy taking form. We are sensing a quickening in the universe, a quickening that we intuit will be the source of our very survival.

At The Light Institute in Galisteo, New Mexico, Chris has found one of the keys for jumping the spiral: her work on the emotional body. She has discovered a technique for quickening ourselves as the universe quickens itself. Like a spiraling galaxy, we are to spew off the accumulated matter of centuries of lifetimes which have evolved us to this point of manifesting our true destiny. During the twentieth century, most therapeutic methods have been aimed at adjusting the emotions, clearing the body, and refocusing the mind. That work has been appropriate to our level of evolution, but it is not enough now. We can move to a level of profound healing when we identify the emotional body as an "entity," a being in itself which has its own agenda. This concept allows us to reflect on our behavior while quickening our vibration, so that the soul, or "higher self" as Chris calls it, can reinhabit our essence.

This teaching about the grip of the emotional body on consciousness explains why we are on the edge of terracide. Because the emotional body is so encrusted with fear, guilt, and anger, it spews bile out into our families and planet, killing all life in its path like a virulent new form of Agent Orange. This inner violence has created an ugly environment, which simply mirrors our inner pollution. Some complain that individual healing is trivial, yet now scientists are invading the womb and DNA with increasing urgency, taking the violence of their dry souls into the essence of the microcosm. What I admire the most about Chris is her creation of healing techniques which work for the present, and which she has then been able to pass on to others by building an institute of global importance. The Light Institute is an energy dynamic, free of time and linear thought; several thousand persons visit each year from all over the world to clear the emotional body and connect with their higher self.

The emotional body, the entity within each of which controls our very life force, does not want to let go. Many have tried to work with the addictions of the emotional body—drugs, alcohol, sexual promiscuity, and personal destructiveness—by means of various forms of behaviorism. Others have tried to educate the mind to control the emotional body. But, the emotional body will always win out; it is more powerful than any person or therapist. It will just shift its energy to another activity which satisfies it, and I think there is a heavy warning in that. Right now millions of people are getting rid of addictions, but we must be wary of where that energy from inner hunger will go next. It could project itself onto a new dictator.

Chris Griscom is courageous and an intense pragmatist. Her ability to manifest power on the physical plane is becoming legendary. Chris's special pattern of approaching life reveals her true energy. "Life is a great adventure," she says. "We are explorers; do not try to prove it, just live it." As a child, she travelled from desert to mountain to ocean with her father, who was an agricultural entomologist. She says he gave her the ability to walk the Earth in connection with other realities, because she was immersed in nature so early. One of her earliest and strongest impressions comes from the aliveness she felt in rocks and plants. She talked to them and moved them around when she heard them request a new location. She also noticed that her feeling about rocks and plants was not considered to be "normal," and very early on she drove these symbiotic responses to the cosmos deep within, until she could find expression for them later. She attended the University of Mexico in Mexico City and lived in Contarero, a small peasant village in the hills of Mexico City. During that year, she travelled the jungles and pyramids of Mexico. It was not acceptable for a young woman to live alone in a village, and very quickly she was taken under the wing of the local *curandera*, the woman who was the village healer. Here she felt a receptivity to her early symbiotic response to the life forces of the planet, and under the tutelage of the curandera, she opened herself again to knowing that everything has meaning. She opened to the God force, as she had done when she was a little girl, speaking to rocks and plants. She discovered again that we move to divine octaves of resonance when we open to the synchronicity of experience.

Next came her nine years in the Peace Corps, where she found form and context in outside experience for her intense, inner ground of being. As a community development worker in El Salvador, she began her on-site work with life and death that was to characterize most of the time spent with native peoples. She worked with child nutrition and gardening, giving the villagers assistance on how to live better. The villagers came and told her stories of magic and the supernatural. They taught her about dimensions of perception from their own magical view of life, and later this would help Chris quickly grasp the universal teachings of esoteric wisdom.

Next, she went to Bolivia, where she became a psychological counselor for Peace Corps volunteers. Her ability to communicate to the natives from their perspective was of great value to trainees. Her initiations into life and death intensified as she entered villages decimated by bubonic plague. She learned quickly to utilize the "observant eye," to quickly see who could be of help or who was dangerous as she entered villages where a white person had never been seen before. She became legendary among the people; they trusted her, she was real to them.

While in Paraguay, she learned to speak the native Indian language, Guarani. Much of her work on birthing came from this phase, because the infant mortality rate was very high. Her work on improved natural childbirth and her own birthing of two sons brought the people to her. In the evening, the people would come for *criencia*, storytelling about life and the supernatural. When she left Bolivia, she ended a long phase of living with the native people, during which her intense, inner cosmic light was mirrored back to her from the people through their lives and cosmic stories.

Chris came to Escondido, California in the late sixties and trained Peace Corps volunteers in cross-cultural communications. She also engaged in some training and study in the human potential movement at that time. With Silva Mind Control, she learned how to better focus the mind and access other octaves or dimensions of consciousness. She attended Edgar Cayce seminars and became interested in New Physics. One great breakthrough at this time was a gift of knowledge from a psychologist, who told her she was not crazy in her feelings about the aliveness of rocks; he explained that rocks pulsate, that the electromagnetic energy can be measured. She was entering into a new level of understanding about her inner process and outside reality—she was discovering that what she felt inside existed in things outside herself. Later, that confirmation helped her to trust her own healing powers. She experienced a similar level of personal confirmation when she became acquainted with a physicist studying negative space-time; he himself was searching for the sense of magical/mythical time that the native peoples had so graciously offered her. This period was a profound affirmation for her about the reality of our experiences with other dimensions, which then strengthened her convictions and creativity.

In the early seventies, she returned to Galisteo, New Mexico, and spent six years immersed in the Earth, living with her four children, gardening, and teaching a bilingual summer school. This phase was a return to her early childhood, a time without society, media, the outside world. It was a return to inner pulsations.

Serving on an international group of advisors, she returned to Bolivia to run a nutritional program in men's penitentiaries. She was already schooled in healing with herbs and natural substances, but she was not allowed to take them into the prisons. Something profound happened next. She began to use her hands to work with energy, and she says that was when the "healer was born." Again, she was discovering that the powers she felt within had real effects outside herself. It was a form of higher energetics pragmatism; an inner belief was manifesting as an outside trust. She had a profound experience with a drug dealer who was also a murderer. His anger, violence, and exposure to chemicals had toxified his liver so extremely that he had not stood up in four months, and he was suffering excruciating headaches. He was being treated by a Korean acupuncturist with a potent form of electrical needles. Chris watched where the acupuncturist placed the needles, and then she discovered she could move healing energy through the patient's body with just her hands! As he recovered, she watched a murderer become a man of compassion. As she puts it, she gave him his humanness and he taught her to reach out with trust.

Upon returning to Galisteo, she entered into a four-year phase of studying and teaching massage and acupuncture. She learned the power of acupuncture to move energy in the body, but she became increasingly discontented with what she calls "props," such as needles or feathers. She was searching for methods to teach people to just move to pure consciousness and let go of ritual and props. On the verge of giving up acupuncture, she discovered the "windows to the sky," the powerful ancient form of using acupuncture to precipitate the higher octaves or dimensions into the body. This phase is described by Shirley MacLaine in *Dancing in the Light*. For a few years, she worked with many clients using the gold needles to access the "windows to the sky," and now she has given up all such tools. She has trained her colleagues at the Institute in the techniques of esoteric healing, and together they work to teach individuals to clear the emotional body, bring in pure consciousness, and manifest their innate spirituality.

Ecstasy is a New Frequency was written by Chris from notes taken at The Light Institute as she trained her colleagues and from talks she gave during 1986. The resulting work is her gift to the world, coming from her years of living and manifesting her inner knowing.

Barbara Hand Clow
Author of *Eye of the Centaur: A Visionary Guide into Past Lives* and
Chiron: Rainbow Bridge Between the Inner and Outer Planets

I did not know death then. It was a foreign language to me. I had never experienced its sounds, its smells, its devastation. I never dreamed it might become a reality which would shape my entire destiny. So I stood there cloaked in my innocence, my trust, and received the tiny girl-child into my arms in order for the doctor visiting our village to attend her.

She lay quietly with me, not acknowledging that I was a total stranger to her. Perhaps she was beyond caring, or perhaps she alone knew she was the divine force that in a few seconds would wrench the fragile ball of my limited reality from my hands and heave it out into the sea of universal consciousness, never to be retrieved again. I looked down at her, wondering if she were listening to me with those eyes which were so attentive to my face. She surely could not hear out of that ear, which had succumbed to such a strange fungal infection that the ear itself had disappeared behind a cloud of greenish-black spore material.

My mind was caught up in wondering why the doctor couldn't just magically wipe it away, when suddenly those listening eyes swept past me, or through me, into some unimaginable void, and with an unforgettable shudder of her body, she died!

1

All in one timeless flash of perception, my brain recorded every minute detail—the shudder, the expulsion of air, the smell of already putrifying flesh, those eyes, and an unexplicable sensation of a weight change in my arms.

I heard myself screaming as I virtually flung her towards the doctor and ran away. The facade of my Peace Corps professionalism snapped. Nothing I had been taught about nutrition, health care, statistics on infant mortality rate, the hard facts of life in small El Salvadorian villages, could ever prepare me for this universal truth. My entire body wretched with the denial of that singular experience. "Not in my arms, not in my arms!" But I could not erase the imprint, could not return to before that moment. There was a profound sense of contamination. All my youthful pride, grace, untouchability dissolved, and I awoke as if from a nightmare, shaken, never to be the same again.

Where was justice? How could God show such cruelty to an innocent child? Nothing made sense or had any value if bitter death was our only certain future. I was still caught up in tortuous resistance, fighting desperately to erase its ugly reality, when the funeral came.

I had never attended a funeral and presumed them to be formalities of self-conscious, socially prescribed events. This funeral was held in the small one-room adobe house of her family, and we all lined up outside to circulate single file past the tiny rough-hewed coffin. She lay there dressed in white, with a lace veil discreetly covering her ear, amidst flowers strewn around her pathetic little body. As I stepped forward to enter, her mother rushed up and gave me such an urgent embrace that I gasped in surprise. She acted as if it were of great consequence that I had come to the funeral. She joyously ushered me up to the coffin, and while violently shaking me by the arm, said, "God has taken her. She is with God!"

She was so emphatic that I knew I was experiencing a message from some inner source. I was stunned. I looked around at all the people gathered there, and I saw with my heart that they were all celebrating her reunion with God! There were tears, but her mother's tear-drenched face

2

was full of lightness. She was not angry at life's injustices or God's cruelty; she had totally surrendered the experience of her tiny child's death to her truth that "she is with God." It was at that moment in my life that I consciously became a "seeker."

To this day, it is death that has been my greatest teacher. No grand intellectual truth has ever begun to compare to the breath-taking power of surrender I witnessed in that village of Dulce Nombre de Maria, El Salvador. As if the fates deemed me a slow learner, or God just wanted to test me on my capacity to surrender blame—the projection of injustice—I was to hold other innocents at the moment of death. Many of them. I had to teach my heart to let go of the resistance, to not wail for a reprieve. Each time, though, there was an excruciating pierce to the heart, followed by increasing capacity to join in the celebration of merging with God.

I learned the meaning of the word "metamorphosis" there. I witnessed and experienced depth of sorrow and pain being released, transformed into heights of ecstasy. Faces of light. Faces of God. Surrender was the vehicle of that passage.

It was the shock of death that brought me to life. Compassion became a flood coursing through my being. It was all I had to give. Those people around me had immeasurably more wisdom and experience of divine love than I. Still, on a day-to-day basis, their surrender took unwavering courage. Little by little, death by death, they taught it to me. Courage to surrender.

With great love, I acknowledge and honor them for that profound gift.

ONE

STRUCTURES OF CONSCIOUSNESS

*Your soul is here
to perceive past the
limitations of your five senses,
past the limitation of the
world around you.*

Surrender and resistance are coupled energies. In linear terms, resistance is first, surrender follows, and ultimately the two precipitate ecstasy. The moment we embrace any of these energies, the torch of enlightenment is lit. It is possible to travel to the source of resistance to uncover its underlying purpose and dissolve it with the powerful healing instruments of truth and compassion. Resistance is a survival mechanism of the emotional body. It is produced through the biochemistry of fear. We resist that which we fear because of our association of experience—experience which includes a vast repertoire of what we call time and space. For example, the Institute uses past-life scenarios to explore the otherwise impenetrable maze of the emotional body.

The emotional body uses resistance as a technique for controlling experience. Resistance helps us stay within the territory of our emotional-body themes. The ego identifies itself through our experiences and never truly desires to let go of them, even if they are negative. Because self-identification is crucial to the ego's survival, that self-identification always perceives us to be flat, one-dimensional beings caught in time and space. We are not. *We are not.* The ego can be released from the bonds of fear. How? Through states of wonderment and ecstasy, it can expand itself into an expression of divine energy. Then we can begin viewing the hologram of the multidimensional self. The expansion of the consciousness to embrace that multidimensional reality is what enlightenment is all about.

The moment I expanded my repertoire enough to speak two more languages, Spanish and Guarani of Paraguay, I found myself inundated with other realities and dimensions which exploded my own relationship to "truth." As I moved among peoples of other cultures and countries, they guided me into dimensional realities which were a part of their daily lives. I learned from sorcerers and healers, children and ancients. I experienced the unspeakable and the holy. The impossible and the miraculous were pressed upon me by the truth of direct experience. I watched my Paraguayan friend walk across a long pit of fire. She was no one special, nor was she especially prepared. She had always done it once a year, she said, to focus her mind!

That first tiny child gave up her life and freed me from the entrapment of a heart that did not truly know others. She picked the circumstance for herself, but she picked that moment in my arms for me. I know now that those eyes of death knew me, chose me, lifted my perception out there beyond . . . for love. I can acknowledge now my recognition of that being, the divine roles we played for each other. I have released her, and I know that we may choose each other yet again and again.

You' re not accidentally reading this book. Your soul is here to perceive past the limitation of your five senses, past the limitation of the immediate world around you. Something else is impinging on you. Something else is pushing you. You are all multidimensional beings. You are brilliant light-souls who have a frame of reference for being out of body, for being in light body, for knowing all things. In fact, you have the capacity within your very being to heal yourselves, to heal each other, to perform miracles.

Our greatest miracle is the blueprint we create to carry us through our lives. We create it from unlimited consciousness, a consciousness of compassion which offers us immense freedom to design the blueprint in any environment and with any accomplices, soul friends, whom we chose. We say, "Yes, in this lifetime I wish to accomplish this blueprint," which is not a linear blueprint. It's not, "I'll start here and I'll struggle along and I'll die." No, it's a blueprint that expands out like a rock dropped in a pond, rippling out, on all levels of our consciousness, in all levels of our capacities to perceive, to be alive. The blueprint has to do with awakening the God inside of us, awakening the capacity to create, the capacity to manifest in all dimensions.

The Institute is a bridge between the unmanifest, multidimensional being, and the third-dimensional physical reality of this plane. We are the energy that creates the opening threshold through which that which has no physical substance, no physical relationship, can find form, can find articulation, can find passage from that great swirling God force into this dimension in order to awaken, in order to bring forth the life of the unmanifest into manifestation. The God force experiences and expands itself through consciousness in form. This is a place where the heart can be pierced, as my heart was pierced in Central America years ago. All consciousness, all technique, all communication within and without is for that purpose, to create that bridge, to weave, to manifest the relationship between that which the heart hungers for and that which the heart experiences.

To understand the process, it is necessary to palpate the vehicles that we can access. Palpating means recognizing in an experiential way. We can access multidimensionally through our four vehicles or bodies: 1) our physical vehicle, 2) our mental vehicle, 3) our spiritual vehicle, and 4) our emotional vehicle. We are learning a new language. It is the language of energetics. Its motion is holographic patternings which allow us to view ourselves and others as complete, integral beings.

Each of these vehicles is like the dance of energies. There is a low and high octave to each, and each has a manifest and an unmanifest aspect. It is the joining, it is the marriage of the manifest and unmanifest that we are coming to palpate, to master, so we can begin to consciously sculpt our lives in a truly evolutionary way.

It is possible to understand the meaning of every flicker, every change that happens within those four bodies which function simultaneously, interdependently. We will dissect all these flickers.

We can learn that the physical vehicle, for example, is impregnated with its memories, with its knowledge, and with all the symbols of its actual matter. Then we can look at the face, and we can see the story, the soul, and we can understand the passage. We can understand the being and choice of that soul as it moves in this dimension, as it is born, as it grows, as it experiences pleasure and pain, as it flows through those passageways of the physical vehicle through to the emotional vehicle, to the mental vehicle, to the spiritual vehicle. We at all times see that hologram, understand that flow by which cosmic law creates worlds. The moment that we stop the universe, stop the cosmos, we enter into chaos, because we do not recognize purpose, we do not recognize flow, orchestration.

The four bodies—physical, mental, spiritual, and emotional—are separate yet inseparable from each other. We can find those portholes through which they flow, through which they come together as one, and through which they move apart. Then, through our knowing, we can use the touch of our hand, or the thought of our mind, or the love of our heart, or the great spirit of creation to bring them back to whole form.

THE PHYSICAL BODY

The physical body has its material structure, which includes all the messages, all the symbols that tell the stories of the emotions, of the spirit, of the choices of the mind. The highest octave of the physical body is the unmanifest light body. It is only through the energetics of the frequency of ecstasy that the dense physical body can be transformed into its counterpart of light. The physical body is the instrument of the soul. It carries the print of the soul and should truly be honored for its part in our growth. Until now we have only dishonored, abused, and upheld the lie that the body is not part of our divine being. Thus it is that the moment of conception creates the threshold through which our divine enters form. What a profound gift given by the body! When we understand this cosmic relationship, disease and death will disappear as we know them today. All disease, all contortion and contraction, all shapes—large, small, wide, thin, black, or white—are expressions of the soul's progression and must be recognized and translated. The expression, "Hole in the spirit, hole in the body," is apt, and must be minded. While the physical body is existing within the confines of the third dimension, the light body—its highest octave—moves beyond to the realms of ethereal consciousness. The essence of the evolutionary promise awaits us in our passage through the threshold of light. And, there is a specific physics of the light body which relates to the quickening of our frequency into light particles coalesced by pure thought. It is this specific physics that we are working with as we help clients experience bringing the higher self into the body.

THE MENTAL BODY

In our physicalness, our third-dimensional realities, we have come to identify only with the finite mind which encompasses our intellectual, left brain assessment of truth. It is a totally linear modality of consciousness. Its very linearity prohibits it from being able to perceive the immense volume of data coming in. It is so slow to process the information that we may not be able to see a crucial situation with the clarity necessary, ultimately, for our survival. The mind, however, is the most powerful instrument for survival we have. The mind controls the physical body. Each and every cell in the body has mind; the cellular mind is a governing consciousness which is a living computer dictating the function of the cell. The DNA holds the coding so that as the cell dies, it is replaced by other cells which perfectly and endlessly replicate the cells before them. The mind gives a clear dictate to the body to perform perfectly and imprints it with the desired state of being. The body will copy exactly the mandates of the mind, and we know for a fact that the mental body controls the physical body. We can consciously alter our heart rates, our body temperature, and even our threshold of pain and pleasure. *Consciousness* is the key word here. As we learn to intentionally direct our consciousness towards the body, we will perform miracles. It is not our bodies that resist health. Cosmic law demonstrates that all living things move in the direction of health and light.

The finite mind, within its linear modality, utilizes only about 10 percent of the brain's capacity. The other 90 percent lies dormant, waiting for the us to discover it. We do have a vehicle capable of that octave of exploration. I call it the "higher mind."

The higher mind thinks holographically. It utilizes all the avenues of perception and realizes all the possible echoes and ramifications. We can teach ourselves to recognize and access the higher mind. It pulsates at a different speed, allowing us to filter through two or three or ten dimensions at once with recognition and understanding. It allows the left and right hemispheres of the brain to synchronize. When these hemispheres begin to pulsate in unison, there is a change in the actual physiology of the brain waves that facilitates a heightened awareness. Most importantly, the higher mind accesses multidimensional increments of knowledge and realities so that we can utilize these realities as tools in this dimension. This is the genius octave of consciousness, and it belongs to us all.

Holographic thought is the key to our survival on this planet. We must begin to recognize all interrelationships or we will ultimately succumb to the chaos we are creating through our illusion of separation because the finite mind cannot encompass the whole. Whales have exactly the same brain as we, except seven times larger. They have made the catapultic leap into holographic thought. Whereas we are caught in our linearity, they use sound as the medium of holographic consciousness and are thus able to digest immense quantities of information simultaneously.

THE SPIRITUAL BODY

The spiritual body is the most elusive of the four vehicles because it is not truly anchored in the material realm. It comes to us by oscillating vibrational waves through the grace of the higher self. The higher self is the megaphone of the soul, the "emissary to the periphery," which allows us to sense that which is beyond our physical senses. The master glands, the pineal and the pituitary, function as radar antennas into the ethers to pick up the oscillations.

The anatomy of the spiritual body is intricately fascinating. Any discussion of it is merely a descriptive nuance, for its domain cannot be placed within linear boundaries. The infinite mind cannot be encompassed by the finite mind. Its interface with our human frame of reference is totally holographic and multidimensional, and therefore necessitates expansion into the higher mind, the ecstatic state, even to palpate its existence. That is, our human frame of reference must, in itself, become holographic.

We speak of the "spirit" and "soul" as if they were interchangeable cognates of the spiritual body. For our purposes, they are not. "Spirit" is the energy that interfaces with the material realm. It has astral properties. In fact, when, for some traumatic reason, the death transition isn't complete, the "spirit" aspect which is impregnated with the personality self may become caught in the astral dimension. These are the famous "ghosts."

It is true that some entities choose to relate through the astral dimension because of a desire to serve humankind. However, this is always a mechanism of karma, an inherently symbiotic relationship of growth for both parties.

When we speak of "spirit," it always conjures a sense of individualized consciousness which we relate to in a personalized way. The "spirit" of any being needs to be a part of the being, even after death. To the contrary, the "soul" of any being is unknown and foreign. We could not recognize a friend by his soul, but his spirit is always familiar to us. It is a palpable essence. The astral body is to the spirit what the light body is to the soul.

The soul lends us no recognizable qualities. It does not truly belong to planes of matter. Thus, there is no palpability to individualized consciousness. Instead, we must utilize the convergence point of our own higher self to that of another.

The spiritual body is like a coagulation of conscious fluid which forms out of the infinite sea of divine source. Like a silent seed, it has awaited the impulse of our distant memories to disperse it throughout the matrix of our interdependent bodies. Once rooted, it flowers. By means of its true beauty, it allows us to see our life's purpose and source. It is a poignant source of our growth and evolution at this time and the only gateway to survival. When we attune to our spiritual body and allow that frequency of love, oneness, and divine universal consciousness to impinge upon the emotional body, we begin to experience wonderment and hope.

THE EMOTIONAL BODY

The emotional body is a body that we know mostly by its physical expression. We can access it through its anger, through its passion, through its fear, through all of those palpable energetics that are definitely physical in nature and flow through the physical body. It has matter, has weight, and speaks the language of color spectra and frequencies. We humans, at our present level of consciousness, have only begun to identify the outer wriggling, the crust, of the emotional body. The other part of the emotional body is a great depth that lives outside of time and space. We must move into that depth, pulling through from the invisible realm, the threads of the emotional body that are not at this time perhaps even recognizable. What has not been understood until now is that the emotional body is an entity, an integral being with its own consciousness and its own laws of reality.

The lower octave of our emotional bodies is experiencing an evolutionary oscillation at this moment of time. As the spiritual frequency is quickening the energies of the planet, our emotional bodies are also experiencing a speeding-up which is producing more spon-

taneous states of ecstasy, bliss, and rapture. We are quickening ourselves, our consciousnessness is expanding, and we are beginning to
discover colors beyond our spectrum of light. These colors are shining,
translucent subtleties of light itself. These are the correlates of ecstasy,
the emotional body of our divine selves. Through the threshold of our
higher self, we access this energy and bring it into form.

It is the coordination and relationship amongst all four bodies
which together create consciousness. The mental body orchestrates the
physical body. It filters and creates, and it is the cell of the physical body
which chooses the disease, chooses the images, and organizes the
DNA to stimulate the physical vehicle. We can use the mental body
to control, to speak to, to alter the physical vehicle.

We attempt to use the mental body as the buffer in all of these
four aspects of our personal hologram. That is why, in our outer conscious levels, we have such a linear, limited perception, why we don't
see each other's auric fields, why we don't see the whole person in
another. We're using the mind as a buffer because of judgment and
self-righteousness, which are the soldiers, the guardians, of the emotional body.

The mental body does not however orchestrate or control the
emotional body. It is unable to direct it, except in a limited behavioral
way. Our experience of the emotional body is like the tip of an iceberg.
We relate to it as if it were only our tears, our anger, our guilt. It is ever
so much more than that. We can say, "I will not be angry," and we can
use behavior modification to bypass the expression of that anger which
we wish to avoid experiencing. However, the energetics of those emotions cannot be stopped, simply because of the law of energy; they will
find other avenues of expression. For example, we will continually find
ourselves in situations where "other" people are in conflict and
angry—witness the whole world—or we channel the anger into self-
righteous actions. Such actions are at least somewhat useful but they
are ultimately destructive as they perpetuate the illusion of separation
and pretense.

We can use the mental body in that way to constrict, to control,
to hide, to alter our behavior. We cannot decrystallize those emotions
or dissolve them, because that part of the mental body operates on certain horizontal planes with a certain linearity that does not allow emotional decrystallization.

It is the spiritual body that dances with the emotional body, creating that special relationship, that allows the emotional body to "quicken," to speed up, so that it moves from its slow darkness into form, into light. We must be able to precipitate in and access the spiritual energy, to alchemically merge it into the emotional body. The emotional body then begins to quicken its vibration by bringing itself into light. It begins to shed its experiences, its memories of the slower vibration of anger, guilt, and fear. Guilt, anger, and fear hold us in captivity when the emotional body is feeding itself on fear, and the physical vehicle, the spiritual vehicle, and the mind vehicle are all captive of that energy. When the four bodies are in perfect concert to each other, the mental and spiritual bodies originate the plan, and the physical and emotional bodies carry out the exact design and complete the circle.

At the Institute, we open the windows to the sky—to bring forth that multidimensionality, that spiritual energy. But we cannot create a bridge with substance, a bridge that we can count upon, that we can call reality, until we understand fully all of those subtle aspects of the emotional vehicle, the emotional body. It must quicken into a frequency that allows the physical vehicle to become free, that allows us to release ourselves from all those mind imprints which say, "my body is fat," "my body is emaciated," "my body is dark," "my body is light." Those are positionalities through which the soul attempts to speak, through which the soul attempts to bring learning, to teach, to find its own light. It is the emotional body that is controlling those perceptions of our physical vehicle. It is the emotional body's representation of the world, its ability to quiet the mind, its capacity to be whole or ill. We cannot go around the emotional body. We can pretend to not have the anger, guilt, fearing, or sadness, but ultimately we must move through those imprints and decrystallize them with our consciousness. However, we can only decrystallize emotions of which we are conscious.

In sessions with people, we begin to make the space for the integration of our divine selves through the vehicle of the emotional body, so that we understand its needs, its intentions, its source, and can palpate the energy of that body and work with it. Otherwise, the emotional body will endlessly orchestrate our consciousness, orchestrate our capacity to see truth by keeping us the captive of our positionality. It will feed us as a possession feeds us; it will keep us on the plane to which it is accustomed.

Our emotional bodies are *entities*. We must view them initially as possessions, so that when we come to the capacity to see them as divine, we will have touched a new octave in this dimension. We will touch the octave of ecstasy, of rapture, a new frequency which is not at this time a part of our reality.

We must mold the emotional body by entering into experiences with it so that we can see that it is more than those external expressions, those external experiences. It is the experience of the emotional body that hooks us through the physiological body, and then it holds the mind and body in captivity.

The seat of the emotional body is the solar plexus chakra, which is in the area of the stomach. Our emotions are registered by the solar plexus ganglia, which trigger the sympathetic nervous system of fight or flight. This alters the blood chemistry in the brain, and the vagus nerve activates physiological responses which actually carry with them an electrical jolt. Everyone recognizes that jolt from experiences where they were taken by surprise—the massive surge of fear and anger which brings us instantly to attention. The jolt spreads itself out in widening arcs which characterize disillusion, shame, and anxiety. The emotional body becomes addicted to these jolts. It begins to seek people and situations which will re- echo the original charge, even though we become desensitized or unaware of it on a conscious level.

If a being has become entrapped in self-hatred or self- righteousness or guilt, then it develops a repertoire that has a particular frequency which we can palpate, touch, or feel. We can see the repertoire in the eyes of another person, through the auric field of another person. If we can see it in all these ways, we can understand the positionality of that emotional body with all its addictions. We can help it to unravel those addictions. The emotional body does not live in time and space; it does not pulsate our mode; it does not move in a linear fashion. It moves in an inward spiral, constantly feeding itself on the variations and the compositions of its own energy. So when the emotional body is addicted in that way—and all emotional bodies are—then it has developed a repertoire of recognition. It constantly seeks that repertoire and creates it at the same time.

If the emotional body is hungry for fear, it sees only fear outside

14

and responds to fear whenever it is present in the environment. The emotional body will contract, it will recognize that fear, and it will grab it, bring it in, and nourish itself with it. Then the physiological vehicle will merge into that manifestation, into that which is feared, in order for the emotional body to feed itself.

And so continues the treadmill. And even though the mind says, "I seek love," "I seek something whole," the emotional body will not respond to that. This we will see this over and over and over again as we watch the players play out their lifetimes, play out the choices they make. The mental body says, "Yes, this person I choose. I want this person. I want this relationship. I want this reality." But the master of that choice is the emotional body hooking the mind, creating for the mind the illusion so that it will help the emotional body to bring forth into manifestation that to which it is addicted.

It is a closed circuit, an unending process of feeding the addictions. The positionality only allows certain data to be brought forth with which to recreate itself. We can learn to recognize those dimensions so that we can stop the treadmill and create something new. We can create an expansion, create an energetic process that allows the emotional body to grow, to experience new octaves, so that the soul can grow.

At this time, we are living with the imprint of addictions and emotional body response patterns from many lifetimes. Experience is the only way to find another blueprint. Perhaps the soul says, "You need to understand permission, so go in and kill a few people, and you will begin to understand the cosmic law of permission." We go in and get out the sword. Many of us are stuck in the medieval times, so we try the sword, but what happens is we are so imprinted by the experience of it—the intense imprint of pain and torture—that we don't release it. We don't let it go. We hold it in the seat of the emotional body, and then we pass judgment on ourselves. We forget that our soul is saying, "There is no good and evil. There are no victims. You are just experiencing this so that you understand permission, so that you understand cosmic law." Instead, we imprint the guilt, fear, and anger.

Then, when we choose the next physical body, the emotional body is already incorporated; its experience impregnates the body's DNA just like the genetic code. So what the emotional body does, first of all, is create a body that represents those lifetimes that it is still car-

15

rying along, that represents those experiences that it has had. We can look at someone's body, someone's face, and we can see the lifetimes that they are carrying with them. The body imprints that information, and then it begins to radiate those feelings it has about itself, saying: "I can't have power because I blew it, I misused it. So I better keep away from power." Or, "I don't deserve love. I am guilty." It radiates that frequency out through the auric field and attracts to you those people, those situations, which mirror for you exactly that which you are most afraid of, exactly what you're trying to get rid of, but which have an irresistible seduction for you.

You have imprinted a theme from that lifetime over and over and over again. And the separation between you and your divine self gets wider. Experience is so profound that it impregnates the emotional body; the emotional body becomes locked into it. It becomes separated from the whisper of the soul, which has no way to continue the orchestration of the relationship, because now the unmanifest is separated from the manifest. So the body on the soul level says, "Yes, yes, yes, I need to come in and chop and burn and rape and kill and have these experiences so that I can understand these illusions." But when it actually does that, it creates something. It creates astral stick-em, or memories, in the body of experiences. The bridge is astral, and it is that astral experience of the emotional body that echoes out, that continues through and impregnates each physical vehicle when we take form.

Now we say, "Now I'll work on another level." But the second we come into form, into incarnation, we are contacting our astral energy, which has weight. It is the veil. The veil is the astral dimension. It is integrally linked to the emotional body. The astral energy carries us from lifetime to lifetime. Because of that, the emotional body takes up its old place, harbors its old stuff. It sets up a frequency through its astral energy that radiates out to the physical vehicle, that sets up the message, that allows reality. The emotional body is controlling the show because of its astral nature.

It is important to see that astral energy flows into the cells of the body. The cells of the body then have that physicality that allows them to access whatever the emotional body is experiencing. The emotional body carries through those messages—memories of fear, memories of destruction, memories of disaster, not memories of ecstasy. The emotional body separates out from the unmanifest and does not merge back in. Ecstasy does not filter through; it only can filter through a light body. Ecstasy is experienced by the light body, not in the cellular memory. If someone starts out with violence, it's because the soul is in a big hurry to shed that so it can get back home, so it can make contact with the light body, and with the God-source. All experience, all reality, is interwoven into a tremendous meshwork, a latticework. Each piece makes sense if you look at it that way. Even the violence makes sense.

As long as judgment and self-righteousness cannot make contact with experience, then we are caught on this side of the veil, on the physical side of the veil, and are separated from the God-source, from our own God-source. So once you are willing to move into the astral and work with the stick-em of it—all those memories of all those lifetimes of experiences—and release it, you are peeling away the veil that allows you to go to pure form. As long as you're hiding that stick-em, you can reach for it and talk about it and think about it and conceptualize somewhat in your body, but you can't experience it, because the emotional body is the vehicle of your experience. We think of the physical body as the vehicle of our experience, but it isn't really. It is the emotional body that triggers the solar plexus ganglion and wakens the brain and says, "Brain, you are experiencing something!"

There is no such thing as the rational mind. That is an illusion. The illusion is that we have a rational mind that has no perspective or positionality. Our mental body is totally engulfed in positionality, and that's where the ego begins to play in this treadmill. The ego creates what it wants to see, what it wants to know, and it calls that "truth." But it is separated from our real selves. We are actually the molecular structure of reality, the molecular structure of the sky and the stars and the Earth and the sea. Until our consciousness can expand to experience that, then we cannot be.

Rationality is simply that which promotes separation within ourselves. And the real purpose of that is to avoid pain and pleasure—to avoid experience. Whenever the mind is attempting to be separate, to hold an experience outside ourselves, it is trying to avoid experience—that of which it already has knowledge. Our block is that we are in a state of denying that knowledge, and it is our emotional body that is creating the state of denial. There is no such thing as fear of the unknown. It is impossible to be afraid of that for which you have no frame of reference. We are only afraid of the whisper of our memory, and the memory is locked within the astral dimension.

We can clear the emotional body, the astral images, so that we can take away the veils, so that we can *expand*, because survival depends on our creating that optimum center. We never will allow ourselves to expand to the point of disintegration. We go through death and life, death and life only because that's pulsation, not because it's ending and beginning; there is no such thing. We can find the center, we can know the self. We can expand to recognize these realities, these dimensions, these increments of information whose existence the higher mind denies.

We don't see the astral dimension at first, because if we see the astral dimension, we see pain and anger and guilt and pleasure and contortion and all of those experiences. Since we are still attached to them, we avoid them. And that is why, in this state of evolution, we have come to a stalemate, because the mental body can no longer protect us. It must expand now; we must move the finite mind outside of this treadmill groove and into a holographic patterning that will free it to identify for us those other octaves which are real: ecstasy and rapture, the frequency of our divine nature.

The really hard thing to break through is the ego. It is like a computer which pulls the strings of the various bodies. In other words, the ego orchestrates the finite mind through the emotional body. The fuel of the ego is always the astral energy. It is the astral stick-em that has designed a form which we call "self." It is not the actual self, it's not the God-self, it's not the real self. It is simply that self which is the computer, the designer of the form that we've taken in the third-dimensional world. Therefore, the ego is in contact with all of the other egos or computers that we've had throughout our various lifetimes, that have said: "You're always the victim; you don't deserve any, so you'd better watch out." As a result, we build a computer disk that runs that particular kind of patterning, and we take it with us from lifetime to lifetime.

The little child, as soon as he or she develops any sense of self, plugs right back into the old patterning. As soon as the child begins to pull away from the mother and perceive himself or herself as separate from the mother, then different from other children, then separate from strangers, related to father, and so on, the child begins to plug into the astral dimension—the astral computer that says, "Here's your frame of reference. You better watch out! You're not good enough. You did it wrong." That's the way the ego functions, so it infiltrates all the avenues of reality. And the physical body is one avenue of reality. For example, if the ego has a little computer disk that says, "You've mis-used your sexuality, you used your physical body for seduction," then the ego will take that in and use it as part of the composite that the body is going to develop in this lifetime.

If the ego has a lot of themes about self-hate or guilt in this life-time, it will create a physical vehicle that allows it to continue its pro-gram of self-hate. It will create for us a body that we despise or a body that pushes us back into those old programs. It is the same with the mental body; we have an ego that chatters all the time. This, again, is a frame of reference that the ego is using to identify what the ego self is.

The ego is not necessarily a negative force. The ego is that which keeps us in the third dimension; it allows us to function there, but it's like one sliver of the hologram, and that's the difficulty of it. It blocks, it veils our conscious access to all those other bodies we've had, to all those other thought forms we've been attached to, and it constricts us. By the same token, as the recognition of self begins to expand, the ego begins to expand. It lets go of the concept: "I'm separate from you, therefore I am competing with you. I am judging you, I am evaluat-ing you." It switches to: "I am that which merges with you."

It is just the same as when we quicken the emotional body. When the ego can experience itself on a cosmic level, on a universal level, then it becomes that which gives form to the unformed. The ego allows us to play out whatever octave we have in our computer systems. The ego is that voice, that computer, which is constantly spinning out what-ever we've got encased in it. Whatever is programmed into the com-puter from the emotional body plays itself out through the finite mind.

As soon as we begin to access the higher mind, the ego will go through levels of expansion. When we experience for a brief moment that we are the same as a tree, or that we are floating in water and we are the water, the ego begins to go through decrystallization. It begins to become a new entity which has not yet rooted itself in this planet. This is our task at the Institute—to help people begin to expand their ego representation, their emotional body representation, so that it can go into a universal octave, so it becomes all things. When it becomes all things, then it becomes God.

The ego resides in the thought-forms of the mind. It resides in the emotional body. It resides within the cellular structures of the physical body. It is a level of small consciousness that is separate from its God-cell. Instead of saying, "Suffer yourself, and then you will be God-like—if you suffer the self, you suffer God,"—we say, "Don't trick the ego, simply feed it something else."

If the ego is the victim and then is the victimizer, it will go on over and over again, lifetime after lifetime. It has to dissolve. It cannot hold the crystallization, it cannot stay with its positionality, if we offer it a new way, a new computer program. It can't be over here because of its experience of being over there, so it has to drop it; it has to let go. That is when we begin to have that consciousness, our God-self. That is when the divine enters.

We can palpate the ego. When we touch a body, we can feel if there is self-love, denial, or judgment in that body. How we deal with the ego is to allow the consciousness to come to that understanding. When we bring someone's focus to that place, usually through the scenario of a past-life perception, it is released. If a person is holding a judgment because as an Atlantean he or she did such and such, or as a Roman something else, we can palpate the ego. Often a person will come in with a Roman body or an Egyptian body or an Atlantean body, and we can, by drawing the light of consciousness into that thought-form or that crystallization of what is being held, dissolve it. We can alter the ego; the ego stops chattering. It will move itself in a different way.

The ego in children is formed through the adult emphasizing the finite mind, saying: "Let's read the story; let's recognize A, B, C." By imposing that linear grooving on children, we are not allowing them to use the astral within its relationship to the ethereal. A child would hold no imprints; the child might strike out in anger, and the anger would resolve the blockage, and then the child could be free of it. But we are constantly imprinting, "Stop, stop. This anger means this and this and this." So then the child begins to slow down and record those negative judgments—learns judgment. In the natural state, the child represents or acts out all that is in his or her repertoire, all that is in the capsule, the blueprint.

At the age of one, the child begins following the blueprint, going all the way through life in different dances and different postures that echo the same blueprint. But it is when we impose a positionality on a child that it begins to stick in a mold. Otherwise the child could clear the last emotional imprint of cut and burn and rape very quickly and be in the light all the time.

But the light has no seduction; it has no matter. Again, that is the difference between the light and astral energetics. The light has no astral aspect to it. The child fills up with memories, is constantly stimulated by the emotional and begins to weigh more emotionally. The weight of all those emotions begins to be that which attracts his or her attention, and the seduction of the astral dimension becomes personal reality. Next comes the treadmill, the seduction leads to the treadmill. Then comes the choosing. We choose to be overwhelmed, choose to be defenseless, and it is imprinted and crystallized in the mind. The mind, then, continues to make sure that the emotional body activates, so it begins again. "I am bad. I am helpless. I can't." And around and around and around. So the mind, then, is building. But what it creates is access to the astral energy, which then radiates out and creates exactly that which the mind has conceived.

And that is how the process goes on. That which we think is what we act on. It's the old axiom—what a child is told he or she is, is what he or she becomes. It is the self-fulfilling prophecy. What we've done is teach the child our imprint, our code of ethics, our intentionality. A child doesn't know jealousy, has no concept of "you're getting more attention than me." A child can't possibly have that kind of intentionality. Although a child may say, "I want some of what you have," it doesn't have the intentionality of, "you get more than me, therefore I'm going to do something to get action." And then the adult says, "Oh, you're just jealous, and you're trying to get attention." It doesn't work that way. If we left the child alone or said, "Oh, you want some too," and gave it, the child would not learn jealousy.

This is a very wonderful idea to comprehend because it is the absolute essence of our work at the Institute. Give the emotional body what it wants, and whatever doesn't serve it, let go. If the emotional body needs to act out its negativity, its hostility, its fear, give in to it, and it will burn through it immediately. It's only when we hide it that we allow its positionality to go on. Give the child what is needed, and the child will grow. It is cosmic law. Feed the plant what it wants, and it will nurture itself, and it will become a full-blooming plant. A child or an animal or any other thing never exhibits negativity. They simply have needs.

But when we give children our imprint, they become prisoners to us and we to them. That's the karmic law. We're not relinquishing karma between each other; we're creating karma between ourselves. So that's what we do in this work. We let the emotional body have whatever it wants. A very important part of the initial work is to experience the unspeakable, to help people understand the unspeakable, so that it releases.

It is better to demonstrate to the child that it can survive anger, that it can reach for love, that it might have those imbalances and that those can move through. You are not your imbalance; you are not your unspeakables. In terms of modeling to the child, if you are out of touch with your emotional body, the child, instead of hearing your words or seeing your restraint, will immediately palpate your emotional body, your astral energy, that is radiating out. You could be sitting in meditation, but you would be radiating orange and red and negativity. The child will pick that up and mirror it back. The negativity will stimulate you; it's like stimulating an amoeba. The child doesn't know what that energy is, but feels it and becomes a part of it. That's the mirror. The child becomes part of it, acts out for you. Then you go into your state of reaction, and the child goes into a state of reaction, and you repeat and repeat.

Modeling is a very interesting phenomenon. It's not enough to model our choice; we must model the heart. That's why we're all here, to learn to utilize the heart, which is the bridge. To model to the child, we must model total honesty. We must never pretend something that doesn't exist is there. We just accept it all, and the child learns acceptance instead of judgment.

As soon as we start imaging to a child on the unconscious level— "don't do this," "don't do that," "show this," "don't show that" —we start confining and constricting the blueprint the child has. It will always watch us and others, and that will always force the blueprint to its lowest octave. Here we are trying to model the highest octave, and the child will demonstrate the lowest octave. This goes on all the time.

But something wonderful has happened in this lifetime, at this pivotal point in history, that has never happened before. We are breaking through the barrier; we are breaking through the constriction of the finite mind and being able to palpate this progression, this pulsation of life/death, life/death, so that we can break that patterning. When we experience ourselves multidimensionally—that we have lived before, that we recognize people, that we know their faces, that we know their hearts—we begin to have the opportunity to make those kinds of changes that allow us to merge on a soul level in our divine selves. That is, where no good or evil or judgment is to be gotten, we can come into these lifetimes at this time on this planet as masters. As all the prophecies have stated from the beginning of time, and are still saying, this pivotal time is when we awaken or we die. Want to check that out? Pick up a newspaper. Look at what is happening in this world. It is not the voice of doom that is descending on us. It is not destruction and death that is coming to us, though our beloved people are dying all over the world because they're misunderstanding. People around us are mirroring for each one of us and calling each one of us to have an awakening that says, "Here I am now. I can recognize who I am." Everything that we perceive outside ourselves is a mirror for what is happening inside ourselves.

The way we can create change in this world—on this globe, in this family, in this relationship, in this job—is right here. We've got nothing else besides a myriad of coverings that are useless to us. Inside us, we have the most profound wealth, the most profound wisdom that can guide us in any decision, in any experience, into the light, into who we are. We are not negativity; we are not imperfection; we are not hopelessness. We are not victims. But we don't experience that, we don't experience our power. So we have to find a way to break the barrier so that we can come into contact with that power, admit we have it, recognize it, and allow ourselves to step forward. *It is time to become who we are now.*

◇

TWO

GOING BEYOND
JUDGMENT

Where there is no resistance, there is no harm.

The mind is the most powerful instrument that we have, except that we're not in contact with our higher mind. We're not in contact with the mind in ourselves that decides if we age or become ill or die. The mind is a wonderful instrument, and it *does* control our physical body.

You are not directing your body because the imprint of all the deaths and illnesses you've had—or your friends and lovers have experienced—is impinging on you too intensely. We know scientifically that the mind does control the body. We can slow down our heartbeat. We can change almost anything. We can feel anything we want if we have enough intentionality, if we are clear enough in that message from the mind to the body that says, "Yes, I want you to be well." If we send a clear message to the body, it will do exactly what our brain tells it.

If you send a message to your emotional body and you say, "Emotional body, I don't want to be angry any more; it scares me to get angry," nothing happens. You can change your behavior for a while, and that's useful because we're social beings. We depend on each other, we mirror off each other all the time. We don't know who we are except when someone tells us we are so and so. So we can change our behavior, but the energy just goes someplace else. The blueprint is not altered because we simply stay within one little space that's safe. "Whoops, if I don't do anything with this then I'm OK and nobody will ever know, including myself." What's going on? The mind does not control the emotional body.

We have to change our emotional bodies in order to manifest in this lifetime, to engage in enough power, to create a world outside of ourselves that is a world we truly deserve. The only part of ourselves that can change the emotional body is our spiritual body or higher self, which does not know judgment, which does not know negativity. When we are able to precipitate in that spiritual energy, then we will have access to that energy which pervades through many dimensions. When we are able to precipitate that into these vehicles, into this frequency, a change takes place in us. We let go of that radiation going out from us that says, "Touch me but don't touch me. Love me but don't love me. I don't deserve it." We get rid of that vibration and something else starts to vibrate out from us. We draw new situations and new people to us, and we become the owners of our destiny, which is truly unique.

So how can we precipitate this spiritual body into the physical body, this solar plexus? For most of us, our spiritual selves are disconnected and blocked by our linear mind. In other words, we think if we pray enough it will fix it, or if we meditate enough, it will fix it. It will not. It will bring only a moment of peace. But we have to actually experience our spiritual nature. We have to precipitate it into these vehicles forever.

When we incarnated and took on the density of physical bodies, we made a judgment about them. We said, "No, I can't do it in this body," since we immediately began slaughtering each other, living and dying, and creating emotional imprints in these bodies. From all these experiences, we have a misconception that these bodies are dense, full of pain, full of anger and guilt. So we began to take our spiritual selves into the caves and put on our hair shirts. We have starved our bodies in every way possible, attempting to get out of this experience, this place, and into the great someplace else which we can't even imagine. It is our great challenge at this time to allow the unmanifest nature of our true beings to be present with our physical realities, so that our form becomes truly the form of God.

We must accept that we have chosen from our knowing, from our great wisdom, from our great love, to be born to parents, to brothers, to lovers, to families, to cultures, to this world, for a reason. We have come to do something, to be something, to vibrate an energy. We have not come to be born and struggle and die. Scientifically, we now know the secret of life and death. But we have to raise up to that level where we choose life. We need to understand that each one of us is here purposefully to give something to this Earth, to ourselves, to everyone around us. We must come into contact with that purpose, with the meaning of our lives. We must begin to see with our greater knowing, with our greater God-self, to understand that we count, that every single one of us is doing something here.

The whole principle of this work is clearing the emotional body, letting the emotional body play out all the imprints, because it will run through all the astral imprints. It will go through it in an instant if you don't provide any barriers. If you don't provide any structure, it will blow like the wind. The emotional body will play it out. People will go into a session and will kill someone that they dearly love or they'll act out something that they carry guilt about in this lifetime. When that is released, what will happen is the person will go to the highest octave. Then the spiritual nature will begin to impinge on the person no matter what he or she does. He or she will continue going to that octave.

Your mental body cannot identify your judgment. You have to allow your emotional body identify your judgment, and you have to let the spiritual body release it. What you want to do is come up above the mind and into the higher mind; come into the octave where you're beyond judgment. And that's an experience you'll know when you're in that place. It's the same thing as struggling and struggling with a language and one day you dream in that language. From then on, you know the language.

The mental body will immediately attempt to identify the judgment, but the ulterior motive of the emotional body will be to avoid the judgment. The emotional body does not want you to change; it does not want you to alter its diet. If the emotional body is raised on judgment or self-righteousness, it is going to demand judgment or self-righteousness in its experience of life. It will even bring you to a rational level and say, "Oh yes, I understand." This is what Werner Erhard meant when he said, "Understanding is the booby prize." We are stuck with only understanding, imprisoned by the concept of our mind. We have to break the groove. And the only thing that breaks through the groove is the spiritual vehicle, the higher self. The higher self gives us the capacity to precipitate in the frequency of our God-selves. It is the power, the energy, that changes, that awakens the emotional body. The higher self can change the feeling we have towards each other, towards reality, how we perceive. That's why we're here—to bring in the higher self. Each one of us must awaken and know that we are our own teachers, that we are our own healers, that we are our own priests.

There's a great freedom that comes with experiencing the higher self. We need to do the work now because all the prophecies are coming true. They're going to come true according to our particular perspective. Will you find your God-self here? Do we need to learn how to do it by focusing on the capacity to materialize, to manifest on an Earth level? Are we going to stop the earthquake? Are we going to stop the spin? Are we going to get rid of the radiation? Or are we going to do it in a different way? We can do it on any level we want to, but the fact is that we are going through a profound change.

Our work is about energy and not about minds. The mental body is saying, "All right, now I will use the spiritual body to release the emotional body." But the spiritual body is unmanifest; it can't be anchored in that way. It seems, in our western linear perspective, to be a double-edged sword, a Catch-22. What happens, then, at The Light Institute is that we start with that which we can move or palpate. We're starting with the emotional body, which we can work with experientally, plus the physical body.

Once the higher mind and the higher octaves come into play, it's too overwhelming to stay with the judgment that imprisons us. We won't choose judgment because that is against cosmic law. However, we can only not choose judgment from the octaves of the higher self, and that's what we have difficulty understanding. In terms of logic and in terms of the normal way we operate, it really does not make any sense—getting the finite mind to do something that's not finite. That is the wonderful cosmic joke: that we try to use our rationality to protect us from something. It is impossible, because the emotional body is controlling the rationality, coloring what we think is real through its positionality. Rationality only means that you funnel something into a place where you feel you have control. But it's all an illusion.

Control eventually shuts down the life force. So it says, "No, you can't do that because that might show weakness. You can't do that. You can't do that." Pretty soon we shut down again. And this is what happens with the solar plexus when we control our emotions. This is why children have stomachaches all the time. They are perceiving the emotional bodies of adults, and we become very habitual with our emotional bodies through the solar plexus area. So we try to avoid the pain; we try to avoid the pain of recognition by just shutting off, which, of course, creates tremendous pressure in the physical vehicle.

Let me share something with you. The very first time that I ever meditated or began this aspect of my life's work was in a meditation group in the Peace Corps, and I didn't know what it was. It was a circle of about eighteen people. They had been my students, but at this moment I was theirs. We were going to do a group meditation. Apparently, they had been doing it together as an Edgar Cayce study group, which perceived many aspects of the paranormal. As the silence began to spread about the room, I became aware of a strange, bright white light, which was so intense that my eyelids began a violent, absolutely uncontrollable, fluttering motion. I was gasping; my throat thrust forward, and my head backwards as if being held by some invisible force. Suddenly the white light formed itself into a wide beam of light and struck me between the eyes. The force of it drove directly through my head, and I had a most surreal sensation that my head had been split in half, and all that was left was a huge empty channel where my brain had been. The light was like a white hurricane moving through. A voice took over the space and imprinted me with this unforgettable message: *"Where there is no resistance, there is no harm."*

It was days before I felt like myself again. I experienced floating sensations, bolts of blinding light, and a high voltage electrical charge in and through me which I now identify as ecstasy.

If you want to change your emotional body, you will not do it in your mind. You will not do it by saying, "I'm not going to let it show" or "I'm not going to engage in these emotions," because the emotional body is not your tears. It's not your anger, and it's not those outer-layer emotions. It is an entity. It is cohesive energy that is part of your multidimensional being. So you're not going to get it by learning not to cry or scream. You'll have to get it with love. You'll have to quicken it into the highest frequency. When you begin to quicken your emotional body, what happens is that by centrifugal force the smaller emotions, the slower energy, begin to spin stuff off. What we want to do is help this emotional body quicken by sending the energy out through the emotional body, by spinning it off.

We have not, on this planet, come to a place of utilizing the emotional body in the way it's supposed to be utilized, because we haven't contacted our divine selves. Our emotional bodies could be addicted to rapture or ecstasy or bliss, but instead they are addicted to fear and anger because those are energies that vibrate very slowly. If you've ever noticed that when you pick up on something psychically, usually it's "that so-and-so is going to die" or "something bad is going to happen to someone." This is the way we work telepathically when we use our emotional bodies. When we use our emotional bodies telepathically, we're not using our higher octaves. The closest most of us ever get to those higher frequencies of emotion is the moment of orgasm. Yet how long can we sustain that? A couple of minutes, perhaps, and then we fall asleep or we do something else because we can't handle that frequency. It's an electrical charge, and it scares us. We want to slow it down. We don't understand it because we're not used to it.

We must now be able at this time push through that funnel of initiation. We must reach to the orgasm. We can reach to the higher frequency of energy so that we can more and more hold it in the body. As soon as the emotional body begins to have a frame of reference for this new energy, it will become addicted to this instead of the negativity. It will become addicted to *life* instead of *death*. The challenge is that the light or the higher frequencies are not seductive because they have no personality, no ego, no stick-em. They have no weight or matter, so we don't recognize them.

Each time that you are going to do something that you're a little bit afraid of or that you have a positionality about—like speaking to your boss—the emotional body and the ego force you into a crystallized perspective as a defense mechanism. "I must protect myself from _____." In order to quicken the emotional body, you have to release that positionality. You have to surrender, you have to let go of who you think you are. The ego doesn't like to do that. It's called dying. Some part of us dies when we go into the light, and the ego becomes frightened. You must help the ego to recognize that it will still be intact, that the finite mind will just see differently when it moves into another dimension. So what? You won't become crazy. You won't lose your orientation in this world. You simply expand it. We have to train ourselves to do that, and we need help.

Getting back to the technique, you simply have to understand the principle. The principle is that you must move the energy out, you must move this auric field out from the solar plexus. The technique is to simply imagine drawing white light in through the top of your head and radiating it out the solar plexus. So when you are going to talk to someone and you have a positionality about it, if you spend a moment of simply radiating your energy out through the solar plexus, nobody's energy can funnel into you. You won't be triggered by the energy of someone else. When you begin to do that, you'll notice that people will start treating you differently, perceiving you differently. If you force them into becoming the pawn in your movie, then they will become the bad guy in your movie. But if suddenly you're radiating light and you don't need the bad guy, they're free. They are free and you are free.

You do not need to protect yourself from your lovers and children and government and anything else. You need to understand that you cannot resist. You can let go, you can surrender, because when you surrender there is no astral, emotional stick-em that slows you down, that crystallizes you into some positionality that says, "I am so and so." There's a great guru in India named Sai Baba who manifests ashes and jewels and whatever. When people say, "How do you do it? What's the technique?" he says, "Well, it's a part of the mind, and when you love all creation, then you can do it too, because it's your creation." So, where there is no resistance, there is no harm. You must stop resisting and move into a positionality of reaching out, so that you are channeling the energy, you're channeling the light in through you, and you extend it out. We want the solar plexus radiating out instead of contracting. The solar plexus ganglia are parts of us that extend out from our bodies. When you move that energy out from the solar plexus, it's like stripping the fibers. You're stripping them of emotional stick-em, astral substance, weight, and matter which comes from the astral dimension, which comes from the emotional body.

You can't do it in the head; you have to do it right in the gut. If you just listen to your solar plexus—when you get up in the morning, listen to it first. Just see if you can perceive what you are actually doing. Are you tightening in the gut, are there bumps in there, or is it open? Begin to palpate your solar plexus by pushing in with your fingers. The solar plexus chakra really includes the whole midsection—the liver on one side, and the spleen on the other. It is important to understand the meaning of the center part of your body, because we need that awareness about ourselves.

It helps to get physical, to really be in touch with your solar plexus. For three days, try pressing on the solar plexus with your fingers. Press up from the belly button up to the sternum to open the energy. Push in the solar plexus and hold that until you feel the discomfort. Then release and push in again so that you can begin to identify at what point your body shuts down, at what point your solar plexus closes. The solar plexus often is contracted. It's a misunderstanding that you can protect yourself by doing this. This is what we do, we always contract to protect ourselves from something coming at us. We cannot function as masters when we're in that position. The solar plexus must radiate out.

Emotions are in the gut, which is the seat of the emotional body, and emotions are being triggered from there. If you just keep focusing, you'll see what the differences are. What does hunger feel like in the physical when your stomach is growling, and what does it feel like when it's not physical hunger? See if you can identify the difference between emotional hunger—when you *need* something—or when you're having physical hunger. Begin to palpate for yourself all those aspects of your solar plexus, and then notice what happens when you walk into a shopping center or into a bank.

The emotional body does not want to let go of a condition; it doesn't want to let go of its pain, contraction, or fear. As we begin to conceptualize the emotional body in the solar plexus, see what that fear means physically. See what hunger or tightness or looseness feels like *emotionally*. Just begin to recognize there's something there that can be palpated in the solar plexus, because we need to be palpating that to learn about the emotional body. "This is hard or this is soft." We can do the same palpation on an emotional level. "This is anger," or "this is love." Or we can do it on a higher level: "This is radiating" or "it's not moving." You can palpate it and get all kinds of data from it by simply focusing in on intention. You can use your fingers as the extension of intention. And you can use your heart. We need to learn how to play these bodies together so that we're not isolated in one body and create an imbalance.

We only isolate into one body for protection. For example, we can live in our mental bodies while avoiding feelings around us. You might isolate into your mental body to protect yourself against your emotional body. That's the way we sabotage ourselves, and we all have this fascinating way of sabotaging ourselves or identifying ourselves, but there's always a kickback. Even when the mind says, "Oh, no, I'm not going to go through my pulling out my hair and getting emotional," you're going to do it anyway because you're getting something out of it. It's the essence of our work at the Institute. We're not going to take away the desires of the astral body; we're just going to quicken it; we're going to raise it to a higher octave.

The gateway to all our multi-dimensions, to all these variable bodies of which we are composed, is through perception. Perception is the latticework of reality. It is the design of reality. It is that structure which defines the limits, the form, the pulse, the color, the texture of reality. As each soul creates a reality, the decision as to whether that reality is an experience of love, light, and God—or whether that reality is an experience of fear, anger, and dying—depends on the capacity of that being to perceive and to recognize choice, and handle the discernment. The enlightened choice creates a reality that promotes, speaks of, and manifests the urge of the soul.

That which defines or orchestrates perceptions is our positionality. It is our experience that creates our positionality. That which we are willing to perceive through the filter is our repertoire. The purpose of the work at the Institute is to release the shackles of positionality, to broaden the repertoire, to widen our focus. It is to allow the flow through all of the body, through all the multidimensional aspects of being without being hindered, cut off, or made stagnant because of positionality.

Positionality forms itself from the astral dimension, from experience, from judgment. At the Institute, we use the tool of perception to discover those aspects of positionality that hinder growth. We help find the aspects that allow for the flowing, for the growth to take place. We help to create a time and place to call in the whole, the hologram.

In our work we draw the bow to pierce, to explore the crystallization of the whole essence of choice, so that discernment becomes an echo of light. The hologram needs to be freed to constantly expand outward. It must radiate outward with the same nourishment that the soul needs to balance all that is experienced through the astral, emotional, and material planes—all that is known and looking for new channels of creation, for new channels of expression. The mutation, the transformation itself, becomes the dance of creation. This enables each soul to have unending possibilities, untethered to positionality, untethered to that experience which hampers its flow, which colors its choice.

◇

◇THREE◇
QUICKENING
OUR FREQUENCY

Survival depends on consciousness.

We are going through a profound change emotionally. For example, how many of your relationships are working right now? Relationships have not been working for the past three or four years. Why? Because we're doing something wrong? No. Because we are speeding up. We are quickening just as fast as we can, because now is our time. We need to embrace this understanding, not from "Oh no, here it comes," but from "Hmmm, let's see what we are choosing," so that we can dance with the great integrity and wisdom and skill that we have on a divine level.

Relationships aren't working, because the energy is impinging on us with one message which is saying, "You're not going to get it from somebody else any more." You're not going to be able to mirror it: It's all residing in you. You have picked everyone you'll ever see in your life, including the guy on the street. You have. When you begin to look into your multidimensionality, when you begin to look into your past lives, you begin to experience the fact that you are, none of you, strangers— *you are choosing all of this energy.* When you experience that, something happens which is very important. The story itself, the content of your past lives, is irrelevant. But the *themes* of all our experiences are crucial to our capacity for survival.

Your body is composed of all those thought-forms that you, individually, have had on a soul level, and all the thought-forms of the souls that were incarnating at the same time all of you were incarnating. If I experience anything, it is accessible to all of you. The imprint is there, because *we are not separate.* So when we have an experience in any lifetime, that imprint carries forward. When we recognize that and say, "Ah, here's the story; here's the theme," we can decrystallize that theme out of the molecular structure of our bodies. Even if it's a "good and powerful lifetime," we must get rid of it. It's in the way now, and we must clear it all.

The second we let go and release all those themes, the energy circles around and comes back into the essence of its pure form, devoid of the imprint of past experience. It isn't necessary to believe in past lives for this process to work. Those things you experienced when you were a child, the patterns that you chose that gave you the cultural, the emotional, the mind imprint—are still moving through you. Teenage children have such a difficult time in saying to their parents, "I don't know what I am, but I'm *not* you!" This is because they *are* you. The imprint between parent and child is so intense that it is as if they are one. The child chooses that parent to be honed, and the parent is honed by the experience of raising the child.

We have chosen our parents. We could revolutionize the world with that knowledge, because everybody has stuff, stick-em, in their families because *our immediate family is our own intense karma.* Our parents, siblings, and children are the souls with whom we've traveled over and over again.

A psychiatrist once said 90 percent of marriages are for the purpose of revenge. Recognize it? So what we want to do now is bring in a little cosmic smile. We're not stuck right here. We can change it, but we can only change it by changing ourselves, by changing that emotional-body imprint which is radiating out to the outside world.

We are experiencing some incredible images at this time, images of possible extinction. Socially we are having tremendous difficulty with our sexual energy, and we're seeing new diseases and old diseases which are a message to us. We don't have to go very far to see what it is we need to clear. Just look around. What about war? What is war saying? It's saying "Stop now, this doesn't work. Let's try something else." This game is getting very old and very dangerous here. We need to do something else, or none of us are going to be here any more.

We need to look at our physical vehicles. We are not using our physical vehicles in the way they were created by our God-selves for use. It is our birthright to walk through walls. The molecular structure of our bodies is light. At this time, we're vibrating very, very slowly. We're having difficulties with relationships, we're having difficulties with sexual abuse. And again, I have to say to you that there is a whole different way to move all of those issues, all of those unspeakables.

We're uncovering our unspeakables as fast as we can right now. Let's look at these unspeakables; let's perceive them as they really are. What are they really saying to us? If you catch my drift about choosing parents, you are not the victim of your "lousy mother" or your "terrible father." *You are not the victim*, and that is a very important statement. If you could experience that, if you could palpate that for one moment, you would become enlightened right now as you read this. *There are no victims.*

One of the most profound things I have learned through the years of working with people is that when people have been abused, we can go back and look for the person who has abused them. People ask: "Why did this happen? Why did this happen to me or my child or my lover or my father?" And what they come across is astounding. If they are now the victim, then they have been the victimizer of that same soul before. Beyond that linear balancing is the balancing of the scales: You do it to me, and I'll do it to you, and we'll keep this going on forever and ever.

There's something here that's even more profound: The soul who is "hurting" them in this lifetime is a soul that they have traveled with forever, because no one else will do it for them. Nobody else is going to dirty their hands on an idea you have about some punishment that you think you deserve. No other soul will do it for you. Your enemy will not kill you, I promise you. Your enemy is moving into the light and will not move backwards into evil or darkness for you. It takes a profound love to say, "Do you really feel that you can learn by being abused by me?" There's nothing but love; all we have to do is make contact with it in ourselves, and then that's all we will see outside ourselves.

The emotional body is triggered by the ego, which keeps us in the three-dimensional world. That's very useful, but we need to watch out, because the ego is always saying, "Look out for that one. I don't like the vibrations of that one. It feels iffy to me. It feels dangerous." It's always yapping at you. We all have little voices chattering all the time within us. Those little voices, then, are separating us from recognizing each other in that loving way, in that cosmic way in the third eye. When we see on the level of the third eye, we can choose. All of us who are on this planet at this time have within ourselves the physiological, the psychic, and the spiritual capacity to use the third eye.

This is not hocus-pocus. We all have a pineal gland, within which are the cells of a third eye. We can see the truth on the inner level. But our emotional body is always experiencing fear. We always start with fear.

This is the planet of the heart chakra; we are here to open the heart. We have come to experience polarity and emotion. We need to recognize that we don't have those emotions in all of our multidimensional selves. So we're in the midst of an experience here, and we need to hone it so we can learn to use this heightened understanding, the capacity to see. For example, if I'm not afraid of you, I can see you. If I'm afraid of you, I close myself down so that I cannot see your whole being. That's why we all go around with a huge knot in the stomach. It is because we close down our solar plexus chakra. I've noticed that some little children shut down emotionally by the time they are two, and they always have stomach aches. The reason is that they see the auric fields of the adults around them. They feel what you are experiencing, and they take it all into their solar plexus. We learn this habit of looking first to see if we're safe or not—who we like and don't like—very early in life. We constrict in the solar plexus. Then we send out the fibers of our emotional body, of our solar plexus chakra, and we probe everybody to see if they are safe, to see what they're feeling, and then we suck it right into us. If we're feeling fear, and our emotional body is addicted to fear, we're going to go out and find some because it's a biochemical stimulus, just like a drug. Fear is a stimulus; it makes us feel alive for a while.

When you feel fear, your solar plexus chakra grabs up; the solar plexus ganglia trigger the response in your sympathetic nervous system. Drug addicts all recognize that jolt; it's an orgasmic jolt. It is literally and physiologically an orgasmic jolt, and your emotional body has become addicted to it. It wants that stimulus and it's hungry for it, because otherwise we feel like we are inexorably dying. We start to create a reality based on wanting that jolt, not based on who we are at all. We create a reality based on who we want to play with outside ourselves, who we can attract in so we can receive that jolt.

We need to discover this reactive principle so that we can release each other. We are ready to see within each other's faces that recognition, that commonality, that understanding that we're here together, and we came to do it together. We don't want to put experience in a box so that we can control it. We want to move now up to the higher

38

mind, move up to understanding the hologram. We have to teach ourselves to understand in those ways. We don't really have that frame of reference yet because we're so plugged into the lower chakras. Therefore, anything that comes into consciousness then has to be run through the filter of the emotional body, which really limits and weighs it down. We have to learn to embrace truth without that filter. When we can do that, we're really centered, and finally we have moved away from the reactive state. We don't have to react; that has nothing to do with our survival. We are then living within the essence of our own pure form.

This is the great lesson on this planet at this time. Our survival depends on our individual consciousness. That's why we have to move to a frequency that's high enough. For if there is radiation, if all those images of fear come to pass, only pure consciousness will be our ally, strong enough to transmute our negative creations.

It is only our own game-playing and our own veils that continue the separation and the judgment and the self-righteousness. "Oh, I am this way with these people, but when I put on this uniform, I'm that way with those people." We must drop all those garbs and start to function in a holographic way.

That is when the new age begins. All those arbitrary separations are not real. That's why it's so important for us to recognize that we do actually read auric fields, that we do feel the energy. We must recognize and accept and honor the fact that we do it and that we're accurate. When we can say, "I can see you. I know what your thought-forms are. You can see me," then we're going to stop playing games with the other person. We will recognize the other person in a real way.

The world is hungry, and we have chosen to come to provide that nourishment. That's the difference between the emerging consciousness and the old patternings of the mind. Even religion, which has had the opportunity to be the most experiential and connected of all patternings, has become so crystallized that there's no feeling in the rituals any more. That's perfect, because we need to let go of the rituals now, let go of the middle man in every way. We don't need the roles and the costumes.

Our work at The Light Institute is about releasing all of the mental body's compartments so that we can go free, so that we can expand into the other 90 percent of the brain that knows what is happening. Then we're never caught off guard on any octave, whether it's radiation coming towards us or anything else. We're no different from the grasshopper or the bird; we just have forgotten. We have that reptilian brain, that capacity to know. Something's in the air; a memory is returning, something's building up someplace. We have to get rid of the chatter so we can hear. We must go inside and listen.

We need to pay such acute attention so we can find that one place where the membrane is thin and pierce the heart. Everything I'm teaching you is based on information that has come from people — from people's bodies and not from their minds. The body never lies. The body will perfectly describe to you the quality of the emotion — not just that this is anger, but this is anger in 27 different octaves: spiritual anger, physical anger, mental anger. When we let the body cue us, then we know how to really see what is going on. Sometimes we let something go, it's not important, or sometimes we focus on a cue. It's part of the informational system that's creating the hologram, but we have to know which string to pluck. Our success depends on how well we can pay attention and pull that string. If we pull this string over here, we get no response or very little response. We're paying attention to the cues which may come from vibrations on our fingers, heat rising from the body, colors they're discussing or scenes that they're telling us about, or a pain they report someplace in the body. If we're paying attention to the cues, we'll automatically pull that one string that will trigger the changing, the movement toward piercing.

As we move around with a person, we realize that everything is tucking itself in and there are compartments. There is no chaos. It's all saying the same thing. Eventually, we begin to enjoy how exquisite the body is, because the body will tell us the truth in every possible way — the emotional body will tell us, the physical body will tell us, the mind will tell us. We'll get the same story out of every aspect of that person. Actually, we already know so much. We just become cognizant of the skills we already have.

At the Institute, we're placing our intentionality on someone and listening. All of us get data all of the time when we encounter somebody, but we generally shut it off and don't bring it into consciousness. We can choose to shut it off and then not know, or we can bring it into consciousness and recognize that it is all a very specific language to us.

We all know the meaning of color. Only a few people may actually see the colors in the auric field, but we all know the auric field; we all know it's there. Just take a feeling you get from somebody, close your eyes, and see what color it is. You would know, if you saw red in someone, that red indicated energy or anger. You can sense whether anger is from force. The yang energy, the male aggressive force, is first illustrated through red. If we see red in someone, we are able to palpate it to see if it represents anger, which is an emotion, or whether it represents life energy. Colors are all interrelated, as the bodies are interrelated. They are simply messages from the body, from emotions. So, colors in the auric fields are universal, they can be interpreted, they are not constricted to our cultural representation. They have universal meanings because the length of a vibrational frequency is the cause of the colors. We want to be able to allow someone to speak to us from the vibrational frequencies simply by placing our attention on them, by listening. It's a real trick to place your attention totally on someone—not on your interaction with that person—but to put your attention on that someone.

Through the process we've developed at The Light Institute, we are able to get in touch with what is happening inside. As a person is moving through a past life and something critical is going on, we will be able to pluck a thematic thread from a particular emotion or a particular thing that is suggested by a smell or by a color. We are present to allow that thread to come forth. The facilitator is a bystander, an orchestrator. It is our job to protect, to not interfere, only to guide. We've had to learn a kind of orchestration that isn't manipulative, that isn't our own positionality, our own interpretation, which allows each person to seek his or her truth and open that truth.

The latticework of the body language must be developed. Then if we can perceive it, the little flag goes up; and if we don't think about it or analyze it, if we can grab the perception of it when people move in a direction, then we will be able to guide them to where they need to go without forcing them. We avoid manipulating them or "leading the witness." We are providing the environment that lets them feel safe enough and free enough to go over here and play with red, which may trigger their sexual energy, which may trigger their anger, which may trigger their pain. We are allowing them to go on because they will be able to come into contact with the great "Ah-ha!"

41

Feel your emotional body yourself. If you are living with fear, which we usually are, the only way to move through that fear state is to contact our spiritual energy, to precipitate and pull the higher self into this vehicle so that it begins to vibrate faster. All colors have vibration, everything vibrates.

If you're vibrating fast enough and you're radiating out, nothing can come into your solar plexus. Eventually it's time to take flight; eventually it's time to go home. Home isn't someplace else; home is our frequency, our experience of light. It's all knowing, that recognition whereby we lose our focus on this one puny part of ourselves, this "me" that we have created in this dimension.

We must come into contact with the *now*, in this lifetime, so we can get off the karmic treadmill. Karma is not a punishment; we don't have to do it forever. We can choose to be here as masters. We can become masters today—not tomorrow, not with the next ten books we read, not with the next "how good we are with our children," but simply with our recognition of ourselves. Who is the self that is using this vehicle to be in this dimension? This dimension is going through profound change now. The Earth is vibrating faster, this dimension is quickening. We can now utilize our capacity to recognize, to let the ripples go out of the emotional body, so that we can experience ourselves as much bigger, much faster, much clearer. The experience of light is not separate from us; we don't have to be only here.

Spirituality is our birthright. We can't search for it anywhere because we were born with it, just as we were born with these incredible brains. We have reptilian brains which we still remember, because as children we functioned with our reptilian brains. That reptilian brain is the animalistic part of us that tells us the second there's radiation or poisons around us. It wasn't hours or days or weeks for the radiation to come in from the Chernobyl clouds to the United States; it was almost instantaneous. People all over the world perceived it, and children all over the world perceived it. They were being hit with a very fast, spewing vibration. The vibration is very similar to cancer in the way it behaves. Once affected, the electrons in the cells start radiating in every dimension. Chernobyl was graduation day. We can no longer subscribe to the "them and us." What happens to them happens to us.

We can tune in to these highly instinctual and ancient parts of ourselves. We do not need to be special, but we have to be careful. We all have reptilian brains, and if we would tune our attention to that reptilian brain, we would be able to perceive on a much expanded level. Our expanded perception is not just on the emotional level—"do I like this person" or "do I not like this person"—but also whether it's going to be a cold winter or whether there will be disease. We're not paying attention to possible real dangers in our reality because we think we are separate. We have gotten caught in our emotional body that asks, "Do I look OK? Am I as good as you?" instead of contacting our own inner frequency. We need to use those frequencies, all of those aspects of telepathic communications. We need to do it all the time. We don't see each others' auric fields because we don't know that we can. The auric fields of others will tell us about them. We just need to expand on our consciousness in order to be able to do that. We need to use what we have. Our bodies are precious to us, they innately have all the aspects of telepathic communications we require. We need to stop judging our bodies and stop punishing them. We need to stop starving them and stretching them in our lust for perfection. We need to stop saying, "No, we can't feel joy. We can't feel ecstasy." The truth is that joy and ecstasy are part of our as-yet-untapped potential.

Consciousness defines our reality, but we're addicted to our sorrow. We can learn to view ourselves in a way that's expanded, that's beyond this contracted, thin, small reality. We change our perception by understanding the emotional body. How? By simply moving to where it's actually living, and it's living in sorrow. It's living in that large intestine, polluting itself with sorrow. So you simply turn its attention and its intention elsewhere, and feed it something else. Learn to see where you're actually surviving. What is the octave of your reality? What's the substance and the content of your survival mechanism. At the Institute, instead of making people go into some misty place of non-cognition, of no ability to experience themselves, we just give them another octave of nourishment. We are helping people to anchor and pull through the spiritual body so that the emotional body is fed a new energy. Instead of hanging on to sorrow, the emotional body experiences ecstasy. Then when we know ourselves, when we move into a relationship with ourselves, then our whole relationship to the exterior world changes.

People identify the problem from when they were children, or from their relationship with their mothers or their lovers. They're not yet looking to the energy source or where that whole string has come from. They are only looking at the tip of the iceberg. They have all of the emotional identification with their lover or their child or their mother. When they we get rid of the identification with mother and child and lover, they contact themselves. Then they go deeper and begin to find out that everybody is only themselves, which creates a profound energetic change. Our finite minds cannot grasp that we are one energy. So we dance down here with our experience of separation from each other. The real anger and experience of separation comes from the separation from our own inner selves, from our God-selves.

So, we just play it out with each other. It is critical to see that the only place where we can recognize our oneness is in our emotional body, because the emotional body is controlling what we're thinking. The emotional body will help you to rationalize any thought around what it experiences as real. The key to all consciousness is to quicken the emotional body. Knowing that it is an entity with consciousness is a profound gift, because we can know who is controlling our experiences, who is controlling our choices. Otherwise, we're forever at the mercy of whatever we're feeling, of whatever we're drawing to ourselves. The truth is, the emotional body is controlling the mental body; feelings control our thoughts.

Physiologically, the solar plexus ganglia trigger the sympathetic nervous system. They are defining what we perceive in the brain as flight or fight, all of those outer emotions which are the outer crust of the emotional body. That changes the blood chemistry in the brain, which controls our response. That's the mechanism which controls judgment and self-righteousness. It's our emotional body weighing, "Am I as worthy as this person? Is this person more powerful than me?" It makes a decision about others on that octave energetically, and it feeds that decision to the brain. Out comes the judgment, the rational understanding, and it's all being controlled by the solar plexus ganglia. Unless we begin to understand this process and access the emotional body, the solar plexus control will always predominate. Usually the emotional body is looming over us when we begin to move inside ourselves. We then come into relationship; we then access the emotional body in a way that causes a change. By penetrating inward, we feed it new energy.

At the Institute, it is our capacity to merge with the person's higher self which helps us to ask the right questions or touch them at the right time in the right place. But only they can make a change. The reason people get clearer and clearer in this work, rather than denser and denser, is that we are simply opening the door for people to pass through the funnel of initiation, the doorway that allows them to move into their own inner knowing. We are not *it*, we do not *do* it, it is all their work. We are helping them, for the first time in their adult lives, to embrace a relationship with themselves.

We're using our love and our clarity as we work at the Institute. We create an energetic environment, because we want people to surrender to the knowing of their own higher selves. We want to help them find the thought-form that they need at that time, which may be totally different from what they think they're doing. One of them may come in and say, "I'm having trouble with this relationship and I want to know why." For the first five sessions, that person doesn't even come up. He or she has projected tremendous energy on the person, and we as guides can't get to that person until we can get to the inner stuff. We channel universal energy in creating an environment that allows people to trigger or pass through the funnel of initiation.

There is never a transference of a person's energy to one of us. Someone says, "Thank you for saving my life"; we say, "Thank you for doing such good work for yourself." At every moment, we give it back. People think they can't find themselves unless they find appreciation or worthiness or evaluation from someone outside themselves. When it's not forthcoming, it is so intriguing to them. We take them into a deeper level where they've never been before. Where they are able to contact their higher selves, when they become involved with their higher selves, and they let us go. Our job is to empower them in that way. If we don't work ourselves out of a job, we have failed. We are freeing people by helping them heal the initial point of coming into matter, which was separation from God. The only energy they need for this contact and work is their higher self, their own soul.

All we are is the guidepost, there to say, "Check this out over here." People must do their own work. We are not here to interfere with karma, we are simply here to awaken them to recognize their own choices. "You are the lord of karma in your own cycle, you choose everything." We simply allow them to see it holographically through all of their being so they access in all octaves, so that their knowing is so profound that they can never ever sell out the knowing. If you know something in your emotional body but your mental body says, "Yes, but that won't fit in this world," you're going to sell out to that conclusion. You'll shut down your emotions in order to be what your mental body has decided is your survival. As a species, we have to get off the survival plane and move into the creative plane where we relinquish the fear and pull free of it.

We teach our clients to direct their auric fields so that they can become beings of choice and therefore create health. They have to create it in their own emotional bodies. All the possessions, all of those thought-forms and negative energies that are dependent on fear or anger or judgment to survive, aren't able to let go to some affirmation that says, "I am a child of God," or "I am a good person." Affirmations alone can't do it, because they are limited to the mind; possessions and thought-forms are not. We give the emotional body a new diet. Without destroying it, without scaring it, without taking away from it, a client learns to simply give it something that's natural, something it likes better. Once someone changes his or her posture to bring in spiritual energy, negativity begins to melt.

The way to work with this new energy at this time is visualization. The higher self is the vehicle of multidimensionality, and visualization is the way into other dimensions. Visualization is the tool, but it's not what contacts the energy because visualization comes from the mind. When the consciousness begins to visualize, cosmic law takes over. It's not resisting, it's not defining, it's not creating, it's not doing anything, it just allows the cosmic knowing to come in, and it creates that. We recognize visualization through the tools of the mind, but only through consciousness is it allowed to manifest our higher selves in our lives.

At some point you go beyond visualization; it's a very creative threshold tool. The more we allow the widening, the creativity, the more the body knows what to do. As long as we can move ourselves into a place where we allow the wisdom, where we allow the body to do it, then it's cosmic law that we can expand. All life moves to perfection. All lives move in the direction of health and nourishment and wholeness and goodness. *Constriction is an illusion.*

◇

◇FOUR◇
PULLING AWAY
THE VEIL

*Past-life experiences
are seas of vibration,
seas of living energy,
which are still moving
within our selves.*

Moving into the domain of what we refer to as past lives is simply a pulling away of the veil, a deepening of that connection to the unconscious being, to the inner resources, to the inner points of experience, through which the soul has gone to understand our power of light, of creation, of death.

At The Light Institute, we prepare people to go into that deep place by allowing them to recognize that their past-life experiences are seas of vibration, seas of living energy that are still moving within their emotional and physical vehicle. They can tap to come into immediate contact with their higher selves, with the great plan of their lives now. That is the purpose of past-life work. It is for someone to expand their repertoire of the ego's understanding of itself. In so doing, we begin to remove all the encrustation, all the encapsulation of thought-forms, of prejudices, of judgments that lock us into patternings. These patternings very often take us backwards in terms of our own enlightenment by allowing the emotional body to dictate the continuation of those experiences rather than triggering the release and learning from them.

It is my observation that humankind has never learned from history. In some respects we have not, simply because the imprint of our own history is so intense that the emotional body takes over and continually repeats it in ever-widening arcs, ever-widening variations on the same themes. When we're preparing people to go into past-life experiences, to perceive themselves in an extended way, we want to impregnate them, to see themselves with the understanding that they are expanding who they are.

Past life exploration is the vehicle for moving into a part of ourselves which needs to indulge in experiences that we could not allow ourselves in our present incarnation. Very often that looming intermediate zone—light and dark—is filled with sexual urges, is filled with whisperings of the lower chakras. It is the "Who am I?" in terms of "I might not be a good person." This zone is the place of all those imprints that the emotional body has laid down about its worth, its value. It is the zone of all of the judgments, all of the guilt. Those are the flickerings that are still within us. They are very present with us, and they have no names, no time, no faces, but energetically they are so alive that we constantly spend tremendous energy pressing them down into our unconscious. We press them down to keep any flicker of them from rising to the service. It is the part of us that is afraid to yell, lest in yelling we lose control.

We begin exploring our past-life references with people by discussing the unspeakable. By becoming very light about the unspeakable, it is easier to accept that we all have that energy, it is a part of our very existence. It is a part of that which guides our choices and needs, limits our willingness to be adventurous, to explore. We need to help people understand that when they move into something that feels like the unspeakable, that they are coming to a magnificent turning point whereby they will contact the soul level.

That is how it happens. When we move through where we are holding guilt, judgment, or fear, we are released and are then able to see the hologram of that choice. We see it not from the positionality— from the urges, from the passion, from the emotion, from the history—that drove us into that experience, but from the wisdom of the unmanifest soul that says, "Go ahead! Go ahead and experience killing another being." In that killing, the soul will begin to understand the law of permission, the recognition that the victim and the victimizer are one, the understanding that there is no separation between us. If we experience a killing in some lifetime, something in our own body is activated. It responds to that, and we get in touch with the reality that this experience is a part of us.

In attempting to separate someone so violently as to take away his or her life, we then take on the burden of his or her soul lifetime after lifetime. It is very crucial to understand those laws if you want to become a creative force yourself. When we go straight into an experience that we have been blocking, then we are able to pull away the veil to see the experience of the unspeakable. Then we move directly in through the astral energy into the consciousness of the person of that time, and we will always describe it from that perspective, from the consciousnses of our victim. We will not describe it from where we are now but rather from the positionality of that person. By moving back into the positionality of the being who is having that experience, we will automatically release ourselves from the guilt.

Before, we freely chose that because we had to, because it was the choice that was available to us. As soon as we go back into that scenario and play it again from the positionality of that consciousness, we have the opportunity to lift off the guilt. It is like separating a membrane that has been holding an encapsulation in crystallized form. As soon as we play it again from positionality, we automatically begin to merge with the soul. We automatically come back into the blueprint as it was given to us in the first place by our own souls. We can let go of the judgment, the limitation, and the positionality of our emotional bodies which were part and parcel with the physical body that carried out the action. It is a profound experience for us to move into a recognition of being the player who was carrying out an action which to our present consciousness is what we call unspeakable or unallowable. It is an automatic releasing of guilt, an automatic lightening of the soul's journey that allows the soul to make a tremendous leap.

When we are about to move into that deepening which allows past-life information, we have be prepared to embrace the unspeakable. As we do it and we see it from positionality—from the choices that we had at that time and in that situation—we will be able to recognize the string, the stick-em, the relationship between one player and the other. We will be able to experience that the victimizer in one scenario will be cut within the web of that experience and will become the victim next time. As we begin to observe that dance, as we begin to recognize that we can play it from all sides of the hologram, all of our attachment to it is released. Our ability to receive, to accept our own selves, is deepened. It is a very profound experience to be able to embrace yourself with understanding that has been cleared of the stick-em of those experiences, of that judgment.

We use this scenerio which we call "past life" as a vehicle for touching our own self, for touching our own knowing, for looking at an experience of life and death, of love and joy, hate and fear and anger, so we can strip those away from the emotional body. Then the emotional body can quicken, can hold the frequency of the the divine, at the higher octaves of energy, ecstasy, rapture.

No one ever experiences a past-life scenario that is not going on now. Our emotional bodies depict those themes, those issues, which we are still working upon, which are still within our repertoires and activating our choices now. Since our linear mind functions in time, we see scenarios in that way. We see the Middle Ages, other planets, cave men, and other historic scenarios and we call them the past. But in no way is the energy of these visions in the past; it is always our present repertoire.

To verify that, we are almost always reenacting the scenario with the same souls. Whenever we come together and have an agreement about a shared experience, we set up the play. The outcome of that play always creates a profoundly seductive energy within the emotional body to replay it again, and to replay it again with the same energy, with the same being who has been in the original repertoire.

That is how we begin to collect and carry forth our karmic pool of personal players, our karmic pool of extended players, which may encompass the whole global energy. All the souls that are here on this planet at this time are part of the same collective repertoire and are working on similar themes. They will then incarnate together in order to massage or squeeze out the essence or energy of those themes, to create reality from that essence and play it out.

A person often will come in with a thought-form such as: "I want to find out what doesn't work in my life but I don't believe in past lives." The disbelief might be in the mind or related to religion, but the energetics of that person's body has a knowing, and that knowing creates a desire to touch itself. At the Institute, we feel that it is irrelevant what the mind thinks; it thinks because it is acted upon by the emotional body, by the physical body, and the molecular coding from lifetime to lifetime.

It doesn't matter if these scenarios are seen as true past lives or as figments of the imagination—because the source of imagination is from our own inner whispering. Any input that we have from the outside reality is simply the flickering of the mirror moving back and forth on itself. If we read a book and some experience touches us, it is simply that we are related to that, that our higher self is nudging us with, "Can you feel that?"—causing a response that comes from knowing we already had. So it moves around and around, on an ever widening, ever-flowing spiral. Therefore, it's a closed circuit. Whatever the emotional body wants to play out is real to that emotional body. In playing out the scenario in the way it chooses, it will release that scenario.

When people come into the synchronicity of experience within the scope of the drama which they unfold, they recognize that it's true. This brings us to an important part about how we at the Institute participate in that scenario. We understand, very clearly, that the language of the unconscious is through symbols, through imagery. For example, if a person spends an entire session discussing an environment, the furniture in a house or some plans, that capacity to coalesce an image has within it the whole of the dream. Some people will go into a past life and will go all the way through it, beginning to middle to end, with all its particulars. Some people will go no further than the material aspect of it, such as the time zone or the particulars of the setting. Some people are stage-prop people, and some people experience past life through emotions. Some people hear it, and some people see the entire thing like a movie.

It makes no difference how they come to the experience or move through it, because each particle that coalesces into consciousness is attached, just like a string, to that swirling, unformed unconsciousness that contains the whole of that experience. If they bring one particle of that to the surface, they will begin irrevocable movement within that swirling, unseen mass that will put them on the path of clearing that experience. It is the upward spiral that will draw out the energy of that experience.

At the Institute, we recognize the importance of understanding this principle. Then we can, in all ways, be supportive of someone who is moving in these octaves, because each person moves in different ways. Some people will spend the entire time articulating every little detail, never coming to a conclusion. It makes no difference. We are teaching them to pluck something in a holographic way and allow for it to form its own circle, to bring itself to closure. If we tend to be very linear about bringing up a past life, we will sometimes block people from getting what they need. All the person has to do is pluck the one thing in order to pull it into its hologram.

Often when a person begins for the first time to go that depth of the emotional-body repertoire, he or she will do what is called kaleidoscoping. Images will flicker across the screen. A person will see an American Indian, and then see an elephant, and then see a mountaintop. What's happening is that the person's inner self is so desirous of bringing up all these repertoires that it can't separate them out because they are so merged together. If we can put that in slow motion and allow each picture to bring in its whole drama, its whole theme, we discover that each of those (the elephant, the mountaintop, etc.) are particular lifetimes in which the person experienced a particular theme. The American Indian, for example, was learning the same thing that might have been experienced in the energy or environment in which the elephant was living. So it is perfectly all right for a person to kaleidoscope like that, because he or she is just moving around the circle of his or her hologram, palpating it for the first time. It is tremendously exciting for the nervous system to come into contact with the frequencies that have been buried within the genetic coding for so long. The person has simply never learned to hold or focus it until now.

At the Institute, people are given the most profound gift in how to hold a focus and at the same time allowing emotion. Energy within the universe is constantly moving, constantly pulsing, so we must learn how to free associate. As we move along, we will see how this flicker from one time period is related intimately to that flicker from another. We initially allow people to do that kaleidoscoping, and we know they may be doing it to avoid something in some lifetime. They have a sense of the unspeakable, they have a sense of danger which is emanating from the ego which says, "Better not descend into this," because the ego remembers what happened when it descended before — it lost its life or had an unpleasant experience. So the ego is not going to let go, because the imprint is so profound.

It is actually a process of allowing people to move towards that energy without getting any cues from us that they are blocked or without triggering anxieties that they're not going to get there. They must understand that each and every single flicker that comes from their unconscious is a profound gift to them that is releasing them, so they come closer and closer to being able to bring their consciousness in clearly enough to see a whole scenario. When they do that in their past-life work, they will do that in their present existence. When they do that in their present existence, they will become manifestors and create something new and unique.

We have to learn how to hold the conscious mind in a way that can take in all the variables from the center. That is how our brain is supposed to function, if it is allowed to function in its natural mul-tidimensionality. We have not learned to do that yet. Not only are we taking people into their past lives to clear the emotional body; we are also advancing the soul, because we are allowing them to hold within their consciousness all kinds of information that normally is unavailable to them on all kinds of octaves. Their outer mind is recording in a very linear way what has happened, and they are taking in the experiences and making the associations with what is going on in their lifetime now. And, they are also learning to expand that consciousness, to hold several octaves at once. They are actually altering their brain frequency. If you put someone on a machine and observe that person while they're doing past-life work, the machine would register that fluctuation, moving into very deep octaves so that the consciousness can be free of this linearity and expand.

The higher self in this scenario is breathtakingly wise. It will only take a person into imagery, into feelings, into recognitions that are appropriate for that person at that time. It is very important to recognize that there is no way for us to ever have a failure, that whatever a person gets is within the design, within the understanding and the all-knowing, compassionate choice of the higher self. The higher self says, "By seeing this aspect of ourselves, we will be able to make these adjustments, to be freed in these ways, and be able to go deeper."

Sometimes people become frustrated because they see a series of lifetimes in which they were born, struggled, and died; when they were peons, or nobody special, and nothing happened. As they go through those and lift those lifetimes out, they begin to understand how profound it was for a soul to choose to come in and have that experience which seems like marking time. It may have been a horizontal plane which allowed for the assimilation of more traumatic, more dramatic choices in this dimension. As people move back and forth between varying degrees of intensity in lifetimes, they begin to understand the themes that are there, the latticework connection between those lifetimes, between themselves and other beings who are involved in those lifetimes.

If we can understand that they are seeing what they are willing to see, what their higher self is orchestrating for them to see, then we will begin to be able to scratch that surface, to be able to guide them into bringing whatever that energy is to a sense of completion. Then the emotional body can come around and meet itself so it can be released. It will not be released as long as it's going out there and it's always unresolved. People have to be able to understand why they were experiencing those things.

The higher self generally divides past-life sessions into two main categories. The first category comes from people who initially explore their misuse of power. They plunge directly into all of the chopping and burning and intense physical body experiences about which they are holding profound guilt or judgment. They go directly into the most dramatic aspects of those experiences and release those lifetimes first. It means that they are really ready to forgive themselves, to let go of positionality. They are willing to go through a death process, because when they allow themselves to see what they have been holding a judgment on, part of them truly dies. They will have a very profound alteration in their present reality, even from this third-dimensional reality. The moment they walk out of a session in which they have misused power, their capacity to be compassionate and to view who they are in the world is totally different.

These people may come in with negative feelings about their everyday reality and discover that they've had great misuses of power. Something happens, something wonderful happens; suddenly, even though it may have been a misuse of power, they have seen themselves in a scenario of power. As soon as they begin to recognize that they had the power, that they had the choices they made in that time, they forget about the misuse. That power begins to move through them again because they've expanded their repertoires. They can no longer be completely attached to themselves as victims in their present scenarios. It changes immediately, irrevocably, how they see the outside world. They'll go home and start to treat their families differently, and they'll interact differently. Their families have been simply the pawns in their movie and have been playing the particular roles that were designed for them. They will be released to some degree from these roles and will be able to treat others in the family differently.

The other category of past-life sessions comes from people who experience being "the victim" during their first series of lifetimes. Whenever we see them cling tenaciously to being the victim, we can be pretty sure that they've unconsciously engaged in the unspeakable, that they have not stood on the sidelines at all. They are going to great extremes to punish themselves for that or to protect themselves from exposure to that recognition. They would much rather be the victim than acknowledge themselves as the victimizer. Eventually, as they go through "I'm the victim, I'm the victim, I'm the victim," that energy spirals up until they inevitably come into contact with the victimizer.

The victim and the victimizer are one, and we don't need to attach ourselves to either of those polarities. Rather, we need to free ourselves from the grip and the limitations of each of these roles, because they are simply roles decided upon freely by all the players—agreed upon unanimously. It is tremendously freeing to begin to recognize that fact energetically within the bodies. The one that clings to being the victim will need special support, special patience, because we are dealing with a very possessive ego that has learned to protect itself from any truth that it doesn't want to experience. We may see very clearly where the truth is, and we must wait and wait, even if the waiting takes a long time. That person is to embrace and release within his or her own pulsation—within the design of his or her own higher self, which knows what can be absorbed and assimilated—what this person is ready to know.

The good guy is a variation on the theme of the victim. Usually, the price of being the good guy is being the guy on the sidelines. It simply says, "I'm special; I'm different, so I'm not a part of this." But whenever people are always the savior, priest, or good guy, they are cloaking the most profound guilt. It's very important to allow them to experience themselves in this powerful way, because whenever people see themselves as priests, underneath there is always a theme of powerlessness—"I've got to be special, otherwise I die." There is no survival. This is an ego that is in a perpetual state of fear, so it's a survival mechanism to always come in as the priest or the good guy. It also relates to the level of resistance of the soul coming into these emotional-body octaves, because the priest or the savior is rarely into life. Priests and saviors are always into ritual, always embroiled within the patterning that holds them to such a degree prisoners that they never have to make choices. They don't want to make choices because they're afraid of the choices that they'll make.

When we deal with people who always see themselves in this way, we know there is profound pain. The higher self is lovingly showing them their power, so that as time goes on they'll begin to exude that power. Then they will break up the crystallization of the priest within themselves. The essence of that power comes back through them, and they become truly powerful in their third-dimensional life. That's what I mean by a closed circuit.

Then the emotional body begins to release its stigma of power-lessness. This is another way of healing the profound pain that a soul has had. We, as guides, would not want to pull that away from some-one. We would allow them to go ahead and see themselves in that way, and very gently, always probing, support the place that allows them to contact a sense of being powerful and being able to release that pain.

One of the wonderful things that happens in past life work is that when you see your mother, your lover, your child, your boss as the bad guy or the good guy, that somebody in your movie—on an inner level—is released. So we always say, "Who is this? Is this someone you have met or known in this life?" We want to know that; it frees us from our patterning about people. Then we can let go of playing the same old game. As soon as you recognize that person, you release them and they know it. They don't have to be the pawn in your movie any more. So that person's soul, then, is released. It's wonder-ful, and this can be a dramatic change.

Usually what will happen with someone who is very central to your life is that they will either change their behavior towards you, or they'll get out of your life. A lot of people don't want some-one out of their lives; they want to continue—better that than nothing.

You attract the victim inside you, because that's what you're see-ing outside yourself. Understand that you have come here with a karma. If your karma is to be a social worker or someone who has an effect on a universal level outside yourself—say, within your city, your state, within this world—it's your karma to do that, and you're doing it for yourself. If you have that understanding that you're doing it for yourself, then you will have an effect on others. But if you're still play-ing "here are the good guys, and here are the bad guys, and I'm going to come in and fix it up for someone," you're mistaken.

The very first lesson healers have to learn is that we have no right to take away the illness or the death of another being. It is not our power to do that. Healers can lend the energy or perfection to that per-son and let that soul make that choice. We offer only the energy that supports a clear choice.

That lesson was very hard for me. Back in El Salvador, when I held the woman's dying baby in my arms, there was a place that said, "Where in the heck is God, and where is justice and how can this be? How can this be that these innocent babies are dying here?" That's what started me on this process that allows me to now speak out my heart-felt knowing that there are no victims. When we can see the hologram of somebody's karma, the akashic records of somebody's soul, then we can understand why that baby has chosen to be born into life and die. All we can do is honor that choice, not destroy it, not blindly try to take it away.

Sympathy is something that's very important to understand. In our society, we are trained to be "sympathetic." But, it's the most destructive thing that you can do for an emotional body. Feel this dif-ference. When somebody's ill or has had something terrible happen, and you say, "This is awful; that should not have happened to you," what you're doing is triggering that person's emotional body's crys-tallization of itself, of the view from itself: "Yes, I'm the victim, and I deserve to be in this spot." What happens is the emotional body cre-ates an energetic that is holding onto that abuse, whatever that abuse was, so that positionality is intensified in terms of that abuse, and the person doesn't want to let it go. As a result, the person *doesn't* let it go. We have triggered that person into that positionality. If we are en-couraging the person to crystallize himself or herself that way, a heal-ing is unlikely; the victimizer has a huge payoff to the emotional body.

Rather than use that sympathetic kind of approach, we want to move towards an *empathetic* approach. We need to move away from pity and instead express compassion. We need to move into a place that says, "Here is what you have chosen, and you can move through that." We have come here to find solutions. We're here to break the karmic cycle by recognizing that kind of truth. If you want to help people, help them understand that they can change something themselves, that it's not punishment. We are not bound for punishment. We don't lose our lovers, we don't suffer illness, we don't die because of punishment; we experience all those things for growth, and only for growth. It is we who chose the movie, and we can change it any time it gets to be a little too much. People need to understand that they're not victims of anything.

You can't change the father, you can't change the government, you can't change nuclear waste, but you can change what it means to you. You can say, "What is the lesson here? What is it about for me?" That's the only thing that matters—not for sociology, not for community, not for the world—but what it is to *you*, because *you* are carrying it all within *yourself*.

If you take that perspective, then you can see what I mean by by saying, "I'll clear this. How can I use it? How can I hone that?" Because you *can* hone it. You *can* understand the most awful negativity, the parents who said to you, "You don't deserve anything, you're not smart enough." It is that *you're honing them*. The honing is not accepting the negativity, but using it instead for growth. All of us are so very addicted to negativity on this planet; this is because we have so much stick-em in our emotional bodies. We *learned* negativity. We need to recognize that negativity is just process by which we can grow.

The trick to that is in understanding that *we're not the victims*. So let's say that something terrible happens in your life; suppose someone dies that you love. You can't control that, and there's a part of you that resists it. You don't want it to happen. You don't want to make the change. If someone dies, then there's a hole in your movie. You're not going to be able to play off that person. Nobody can take the place of your mother. Your father can remarry, and you can have another mother, but she's not going to play that role for you, even if she does all the things externally that mothers do. She won't have the same energy. No one ever takes the place of that one person. So instead of trying to fill the unfillable hole, what we want to understand is that each experience that comes to us—whether we consider it negative, threatening, or whatever—we can let go into.

As I was saying with the solar plexus, move your energy into that part of your body. Move your energy into saying, "What shall I create of this? What am I going to do with this?" If you lose your job, get another one. There is an expression that says when the door is shut, the window opens. It means that the only one who is shutting any door is your higher self. Why? Always for your growth and wellbeing.

We're very habitual beings; we're stuck in our habits. We truly are, and we fall asleep because of that. Sometimes we tarry too long— perhaps too many lifetimes repeating the same theme. So finally, here you are repeating it again, and your higher self says, "No, you've forgotten this increment here, this aspect of this hologram, and I'm going to help you get to it." So you decide to do what I call the cosmic dance. What you want to do with that is understand, embrace the theme, for your higher good.

Some people just say, "See, I know I can get it." Maybe you're not supposed to get the theme. When you start listening to your inner self, you have no idea what you're supposed to get, so the effort is need- less. All of your ego's attachment to questions of how to find yourself starts to fall away. You begin to see more and more clearly. You begin to be able to make clearer choices for yourself, because you're making all the choices for yourself in the first place. Your higher self is simply saying to you, "Use it." Don't fall asleep and say, "Gee, I'm the victim and that's it and I hate it." Instead, say to yourself, "Where is this taking me? Do I need to move to another place?"

We have so many tools, and we don't use them. If you are unhappy in the town you live in, maybe you need to find out if this place has the right frequency for you. Maybe you need to move to another place. Let go. You can never lose anyone. If someone dies or you choose not to continue with a person or they choose not to con- tinue with you, you can't lose them. They're always a part of you because they're part of your soul's choice. We have to begin to palpate that understanding instead of ranting and raving because someone pushed us off. Let them go. Let them lose the crystallization of the intensity of the physical body. Let them go into their essence. Let them go into their divine-soul form, and then you'll be so close there will be no separation.

We have to understand these veils that we have created through the limited linearity of our consciousness. Once we start surrendering in even the little ways, allowing our inner selves to guide us, it really changes our perspective of what we've chosen and what our life is about. One of the major things that happens is that we hold on when it's not good for us to hold on. Not only that, it's not good for those around us. We say, "Oh, I love my mother so much, and I can't stand it that she's gone." My mother died several years ago, and when she died, she came into my house, and the whole house filled with light.

This is the planet of the heart chakra. It's not the only planet; it's not the only aspect of reality, but we are here dealing with the heart chakra. To deal with it, we have to bring down the knowing which gets stuck in the throat. How many of us speak our heart? How many of us have the courage to speak our knowing? It is because the judgment and the self-righteousness get in the way, and these energies are held in the throat.

Our seduction—a major word in our lives now— to being the good guy is profound. We'll abdicate our power or our realities or our whatever to represent ourselves as good guys. That's where self-righteousness comes from. Self-righteousness really comes from an unconscious, unspeakable place where we recognize guilt. So to cover the guilt, we become the good guys. Then we pat ourselves and say, "See, I'm not the bad guy. I'm the good guy. The bad guy's out there." It's a survival trick. That's all it is, a survival trick. We don't need it.

Self-righteousness is a survival mechanism just as is anger. Anger is nothing but a defense mechanism, and always beneath anger is fear. Look at the people in your lives who are the ones that scream, who are the ones that are angry. Look, probe them outside of your emotional body, and you will palpate an exquisite and painful being that simply needs to understand that it's not going to be gobbled up. That's the defense mechanism which takes place.

Judgment is the same. Judgment is just a misunderstanding; it's a limitaton of consciousness. Self-righteousness and judgment always go hand in hand. It is always that positionality of "I'm going to make it OK. I'm the good guy and then there's the bad guy. There are those out there who deserve the judgment because they did it wrong." I know that this is a tremendously difficult concept to accept, but other people didn't do anything that you didn't allow them to do. It is impossible from a cosmic perspective for it to happen any other way, *impossible*. And as soon as you begin to explore the recognition that you have lived and died, that you do live, that you do manifest, then you don't need that defense mechanism any more.

In one of my past lives, I was an Egyptian priest. I always laugh when people get self-righteous about having been in Egypt or having been in Atlantis, because my perspective on both those places is that they were both focal points of great misuse of personal power. In this particular one, I was a young priest, a young pharaoh, dearly beloved by everyone. I had many wonderful capacities. I could speak with animals and hear them; I understood herbs. I had gone through initiations before, and so I had garnered that information, that knowing, and brought it through in that lifetime. I had recognized from the beginning that I was going to be a great pharaoh who was going to lead the people to new levels of understanding.

I was very confident as I approached my final initiation. I had a teacher who had been with me since my early childhood. He was my most beloved to my heart, had taught me everything, and had always been by my side. I was emotionally attached to this teacher.

When it came time for initiation, my eyes were elaborately painted with pulverized turquoise and lapis stone to protect and guide my "vision." I was sent into the chamber of initiation, and I sped through the steps of initiation until the last crucial test. This was "the discernment of the way." There were two paths, and I was to choose which path. My heart knew instantly when I saw the left path that it was the one. Just at that moment when I was to say, "It is the left path," the face of my teacher, my beloved teacher, came to me, and the face said, "It's the path to the right." My teacher was my life, my only association with any love on an emotional level in that lifetime. I totally trusted his great wisdom, so I immediately said, "It's the right path." The result was death.

You know what that's about? You must choose your all-knowing, even if there's nobody around you to tell you it's the right answer. That teacher had been preparing to take me out in that way my whole lifetime, because I was destined to bring forth a religious understanding that was advanced for the times. So they just took me out because they knew that I would advocate my power. The problem wasn't my love for that teacher; it was that I saw him as the fountain of wisdom, as God, instead of myself. I had known the answer.

When I saw that lifetime, something happened inside me, and I stopped caring about someone else's judgment, whether I was this or that, had the degrees, had the authority. I didn't have to try. It wasn't a defense mechanism. It just stopped me; my body knew it. My body had experienced the death, and it wasn't a pleasant one. It was because I abdicated my knowing.

That's how this kind of work helps you. When you see a theme and you recognize how you have done it in this lifetime, or how you're continually doing it, then it stops. I didn't have to try. It stopped, and I don't have to do that any more. I'm willing to be wrong. I'm willing to fall on my face and know that even if the answer seems wrong to others, it is going to teach me about my divine nature. I'll accept that path now, by myself.

I do not recommend that you work on specific past lives alone. There's a good reason for that. Each lifetime we have creates an emotional dynamic, and that emotional dynamic activates something that can be palpated. It is astral energetics, and you can feel it, you can stick your hand in the auric field and feel it. It has a stick-em. That's the best word for it. It's sticky and has weight, matter, and energy. Believe me, it has energy. If you go into a past life on your own, perhaps you will encounter your unspeakables in the past life. You're going to unleash around you an astral energy that you may not be able to deal with. Why would you do it on your own except to save money or not have to tell anybody who you are?

By cosmic law, everything goes out and comes back, whether it's money, power, or love. You have to let go, or you don't get it. The unspeakable is the same. When we have cleared ourselves enough to be willing to look and recognize that we see each other, we won't be hiding from each other, we will indeed enter the new age. You're not going to sit there holding your negative thoughts when you know that I can really see you. You're going to move. You're going to make those changes that are necessary, and that's where we need to be. Each of you needs to explore and expand and quicken any time in any direction, whether that's through a church, or a counselor, or help in any way. It's appropriate to do that, to find out who you are.

Past lives are not a place where you can play by yourself, because there is such a thing as the astral dimension. It is not in time and space; the astral dimension is in simultaneous space. The astral dimension is with you as you read this book. All of your past lives are popping out; they're sticking out everywhere. That's how we know who we know, because we've seen them before. So the astral dimension is energy; it is full of thought-forms, and it is full of entities, poltergeists, and all kinds of things. There's the old idea of the boogie man. Children love the boogie man because they know he is real. He *is* real. So when you go into the astral dimension, you're exposing yourself to all those energetics, whether they're thought-forms or astral entities. They're there, and they're real, and if you have a particular fear or a particular attraction about something, you are likely to attract that energy. You're going to pull that energy right through the astral dimension and into this third-dimensional time and space, and you will not like it. So it's not appropriate to play in all these force fields alone.

It's not that all past lives are terrible. It's not that the astral dimension is bad, and the boogie man is there, and something's going to get you. Physicists are beginning to explore the fact that there's something on the other side called negative-space time. There's something on the other side of reality.

Do past-life work. Past-life work is wonderful. Do it for two reasons. One is to release yourself from this baggage that you're carrying along with you. Get rid of it. You're not going to clear it unless you do it yourself. If somebody else reads your past lives for you, it might help you behaviorally. You might say, "Oh, that's why I feel this way about something," and it will help to some degree. But you can't clear it that way. It will just stay in your mental body, and you'll make a judgment. You'll say, "I hate that past life" or "I love that past life," which means you're still carrying around that garbage with you, and you're still on that treadmill. You want to get rid of it, even if it is a great past life. You want to move it. You want to dematerialize it into its essence form, so that the energy can come through this physical vehicle, which changes who you are in this world and what you can accomplish.

So don't be stingy, don't be squeezing; go ahead and find someone to help you and do past lives. Do it with someone who is going to help you clear the energetics, the stick-em, and get that away from your body so that your body begins to vibrate as a light body. We can break through the limitations that we have, and it is time for us to do that now. We can't do that while we're hiding. We can't do it.

When you go into a past life for yourself, you're going to understand the consciousness that you had at that time. It had to be OK for you to do it, or you wouldn't have done it. Your soul knew what was going on, it gave you a blueprint that you could follow. When you go back in there, you say, "Here I was doing this and this and this," and what happens is a tremendous relief comes over you, because you understand the consciousness of that being that you were. That being had a reason for doing whatever it was doing. It did, and it made sense. By recognizing that, you can clear the guilt from yourself, you go free. The second reason is that when we explore our inner reaches, we discover ourselves actually to be the kind of people we also wish we were. We find we were healers, teachers, and beings with talents, that we were worthy of love and loving, and capable of choosing lives of great power in the great cosmos. Our frame of reference for compassion and unconditional love expands.

◇

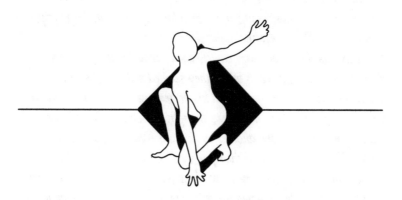

It was time to go home after serving in the Peace Corps. It had been such a long time since I had lived in the United States. Almost a decade had come and gone, and I had lost the edge on the meaning of the word "American." In this country, Bolivia, the issues were straightforward—life, death, food, children. But in the world of the diplomats, I was expected to carry the banner of my country, to articulate, promote, and defend the American perspective. In truth, I had experienced too much proximity to raw existence to maintain any illusion of distinction between an "American" body and a "Bolivian" body. The ultimate course for each one was the same. True, I felt slight embarrassment for my obvious inability to explain or justify the politics or trends of the U.S., and I knew I must return to "The Land of Plenty."

I moved with an expectant heart towards the plane bound for Miami. As I entered, I looked down the long rows at the sea of faces, and a great percentage of the passengers were Americans. I should have been feeling a sense of elation, but instead I suddenly felt heavy and lifeless. I glanced around at the energy fields, and instantly my entire body registered extreme alarm. In contrast to the blue sky visible out the plane windows, the cabin *was filled with a dense, smoky energy. I had seen that energy before. I began to look intensely at my fellow passengers. Ill-health, depression, cancer, addictions were oozing out of the auric fields of almost everyone. Was this what we were manifesting in the great land of America? I was gripped with anxiety. These were the living dead!*

It was as if each one were entirely encapsulated within a cocoon. People were not talking to each other; they seemed sedated. As I passed up and down the aisles, no one raised his or her eyes to meet mine. We were traveling together. Even though we thought ourselves strangers, we were inextricably bound to one another by this impervious metal membrane in the sky. Whatever was to be their fate was also mine. I felt the "stick-em" of that half life descend on me as if a heavy fog were rolling in. There was no escape. I had often ignored the reality of auric fields intermingling, but here I didn't have to look at it; I could sit with my eyes shut and feel it pressing in on me. No way out. These people were not living, they were merely existing. I felt I was being sentenced to that smoky plane of existence. Profound loneliness engulfed me.

As if I were looking for someone to console me, to convince me it was all a dream, I began pacing the aisles again. It was then that I saw her. I could say that she had blonde hair, blue eyes, and was about six years old, but truthfully, I didn't notice that right away. What I noticed was her sparkle. She was alive, all the way alive! She looked up at me and stared unabashedly into my eyes without a wobble. She took me in. She saw me completely, and I knew it. I found myself shaking a little inside, like you do when you've been in a fear state and suddenly you relax. The letting-go causes a slight trembling. I walked past her many times on that flight. We talked to each other with our eyes. I felt such recognition from her, such profound compassion. I knew I was in the presence of a teacher, a very wise soul, a loving friend. She did not know fear.

I had forgotten I had a choice. She wasn't one of the living dead, and neither was I. She didn't have to convince anyone of what she knew, yet it was clear that she knew it all, and her smiling eyes conveyed the strength in that knowing!

We passed through customs in Miami, and as she walked away with her parents, she turned and gave me one last look, as if to say: "Don't forget." I had arrived home—perhaps for the first time ever.

FIVE

EXPANDING OUR PERCEPTUAL FIELD

There are no innocent parties,
no "them and us," no untouchables—
the initiation is about
expanding the perceptual field
so that we can witness the divine purpose
in what is so seemingly adverse to us.

The aura of the living dead is created by entrapment in the realities of the lower energies. Because our perceptions are limited to these octaves, we are prey to addictions and other circumstances that perpetuate the entrapment and the perception we have of ourselves as limited, imperfect beings.

In truth, we draw these experiences to ourselves—be they addictions, imbalances, emotional crises, or physical ailments—as an important part of our soul's teaching. If we can perceive them as such, it enables us to use them as an exquisite opportunity to heal ourselves, expand our consciousness, and move closer to the actuality of perfection. We are not our imbalances. Removing ourselves to a distance from which we can explore their sources and functions within the hologram of our soul's design enables us to find humor in the drama, light in the darkness—and once in the light, dissolve our imbalances into nothingness. Instead of remaining insulated and encapsulated in distorted realities, we must move into higher octaves of perception, that not only afford us a glimpse, but allow us energetic environments which initiate our healing.

The Earth itself is a great source or vehicle through which we can experience pure, divine energy, or *shakti*. The Earth is an extension of our own living organism and is in no way separate from ourselves. It is a body which exudes palpable energy frequencies that we can utilize for our own inner alignment.The Earth has energy meridians called ley lines, which are analogous to the energy lines in the body with which acupuncturists work. Around the globe, there are places which are on energy vortices, or intersections of these ley lines, that relate to the energies of the Earth, the energies of the people, and to the Earth as it relates to the universe. Vortices are places on Earth which respond to galactic energy, and they are very profound for our consciousness. We should seek them out. There are certain vortices where the Earth is sending off energy or drawing in energy that causes it to be aligned, to balance within its own self and within the medium of the galaxies.

If our bodies are afflicted by physical or emotional imbalance, we can choose areas of the Earth which are negative ion generators that automatically make us feel better by simply being in the vicinity of the negative ions. Mountains, forests, streams, waterfalls, and the sea are all such places. Water is a profound conductor of energy, and by simply submerging the body in it, we can effect a release of the static electricity which so disturbs our nervous system and confuses our perceptual abilities. There are magnificent natural centers of shakti where rejuvenating, empowering energies spill forth. Sitting on the rim of the Grand Canyon or at the foot of a geyser at Yosemite can inspire us to forget ourselves and take in the grandeur of our world. The Earth is filled with incredible power spots, some of which are still within the realms of solitude, and some upon which humans have built their temples from the dawn of time. Often, each succeeding civilization astutely placed its center of worship upon the ruins of one before it in profound reverence for the energy so easily palpated at that spot.

We are not different from anything else on Earth. We're not separate from the tides that are pulled back and forth by the moon. The water in our bodies moves with the tides. We are a part of it all. If we go to a place that has a vortex, we can feel the energy. We can use it to trigger the recognition and the experience of infinity, to get out of our finite minds. We can experience an energy that can nourish us, that can expand us into our multidimensional selves.

When we go someplace, on a vacation, we should look for places that have vortices. Our emotional bodies will let go when we enter into a frequency that's higher than our own. The emotional body quickens to the frequency of that vortex. In that space, in that understanding, we expose ourselves to our multi-dimensionality which

70

would normally not be a part of our consciousness. It is very important to understand that the Earth is a living entity, experiencing all that we are. We don't even have to go to a specific place to seek out energy vortices, because we actually live on the whole Earth, although we have forgotten. We don't even have to go into the astral dimension— that's where we go when we go out of the body— but we can project the mind, this great mind that we all have, out there and draw in an energy that is nourishing. We are not entrapped in our bodies, in location or time. We are not entrapped in the positionality of our individual lives. If we need the energy of a mothering vortex, we can just stop, go in, and focus on it and quicken with the frequency. At first, we may need to remember the experience of the vortex energy in a special place we have visited, and then once we recognize the frequency, we can just trigger it. This same technique of attuning to location frequencies is used to locate time frequencies and is the same mechanism by which the holographic mind must locate "past lives."

As we work with past lives, it is important to understand that our consciousness is focusing on the energetics arising from their release. That is why we pay so much attention to clearing the auric field—so that the person brings all the bodies back into a meshwork that is lighter, freer, more fluid and flexible.

The energetics are very important. We do not want people to do it in their heads. Very often in the middle of a session, a person will get a pain in the physical body, or begin to sob, because that which has been encapsulated is suddenly broken free. Sometimes the higher self will help the person pay attention, help hook that little thread from the swirling unconscious by using the physical body. The higher self will speak to the person through the body, e.g., there may suddenly be a pain in the right shoulder. This is a body-language cue about the burden of manifesting. The facilitator will have the person go into that part of the body and see what images are there. As those images come forth, the auric field ripples out the releasing of that encapsulation or memory, and the emotional body begins to astringe and spew. The pain may have been there for twenty lifetimes or twenty years, and it can go and never come back.

Among the thousands of people I've worked with, there only have been one or two who have shared the same space. Most people will identify with Christ-energy or Hitler-energy or somebody else's for a moment, but then as they start to move to it, as it takes on form or matter, they will identify themselves at the fringe of it. They will start out carrying a cross, and then discover that they were one of the disciples. They move into the third-dimensional experience of it simply because they can't take the intensity of the initial experience. It is because of that intensity that the emotional body has created so many addictions. Addictions are behavioral mechanisms which keep the vibrational frequency low. That point where we access the unmanifest is still too high in frequency, and so we create addictions to keep the vibration low in order to distract ourselves.

There is something about famous people that is important to understand. Whenever someone incarnates with a global blueprint, the intention is to wrench the planet through some experience, some knowing or action, that multitudes of souls have agreed upon. Very often the soul which carries the karma of that global work is an active part of the collective consciousness, and many souls will funnel in to garner that experience. Why should each soul go through that experience when one person is willing to do it, and it is an experience that has global content or influence? What happens is that thousands of souls participate in the formulation of that one being, that one body. We have a common access, we're all in body here. We're all using the same kind of vehicle, the same instrument, every one of us. We all have male-female cells within us, so there is no octave from which we cannot tap into another being. In the very near future, this will become a commonality.

Once we move on to the understanding that we are very accessible to each other, we won't have any more wars or any more deception. We won't have any of these things, because they are useless. We have been so invested in emotional bodies that think, "I must be this personality, and this personality is all there is of me." As we begin to help people to recognize that they are holograms, they become more accessible to each other and more easily able to experience the whole. They need not experience fear. The emotional body is invested in feeling that if someone else is around, it won't survive.

As we begin to open the scenarios of what we're calling past lives, we're opening that multi-dimensionality. When people begin to understand that they access each other as one being, they will experience the oneness of being. That will change our ability to see each other's auric fields or to tap into each other's consciousness. The term "past lives" is a misnomer. We only use that term because it's a hook, a string people can pull. They can see it in a linear way. It's an experience of multi-dimensionality in a linear format. The finite mind has not exercised its capacity of consciousness or extended consciousness, but it can relate easily to multi-dimensionality through the vehicle of past lives. It can go in there without going into chaos and losing itself. It can delineate, "This is Roman times," and be able to absorb and assimilate the energy that's there.

We've found that certain souls have predilections to certain dimensions, so when people say you're an old soul, they're referring to the fact that you have been around in a particular dimension for a long time. Some souls will continue to choose to come over and over again, while some souls will choose to go over and over again to Saturn or some other place. When people begin to clear their lifetimes on an Earth-plane level, they often come to a place where they have cleared most of the themes, and they start clearing other levels. They begin working on galactic levels, or they begin going through dimensions. Then the whole format really changes. What's so beautiful about the past-life scenario is that it is very clear; it's linear, and yet it allows people expansion of consciousness. This work can actually effect a change in people's consciousness levels, in their brain's capacity to uncover those pieces of information, and let them all reorganize.

Past-life work helps us to recognize our connections to each other. Initially, we will remember the lifetimes that are involved in the themes most intimate to us; then we begin to become more and more impersonal as we clear. If a lifetime we shared with another had an imprint, if we remember the other in that context, some part of us will dwell with the other in that context this time. Thus we come into those interesting aspects of karma—how we see one another. That's why one person falls in love with someone, and everyone else whispers, "How are they even in the same place with each other? They are no more alike than the man on the moon." But open their perceptual fields, and they show you how they're interwoven. They are forever interwound until they bring that lifetime up, and they shake it around a bit and clear it. It allows both people to assimilate completely what they are experiencing with and for each other, and reshape it in any way they want. That's creation. The more conscious we become of our capacity to do that, the more beautiful our creation.

Creation is ongoing, and each time something is created, it triggers a response in the universe. That's where action and reaction carry out an unending pulsation that keeps the flow going through eternity. There is, within all that movement of the eternal pulsation with all the ever-changing, ever-creating patterns that are going on, a center. Our multidimensional soul has that center; it is enlightenment. What we mean by enlightenment is our capacity to receive, to see the latticework. Just as everything about us is interwoven in all of these interdimensional realities, the center of the latticework is multidimensional and it's integral. Unfortunately, at this time, the only part of us that we consider integral is our personalities.

I had a client who said, "It seems to me that it is my same personality that is running through all my lifetimes. I seem to be the same through all my lifetimes." I helped her to understand that what was the same was her soul. She was beginning to palpate that thread of the "I Am," the soul. It is a fluidity of consciousness and connectedness. We will grasp it as we move more and more through multidimensional experiences.

It's the same as the first time we hold a flower in our hands and someone says, "Now we're going to do the exercise of becoming a flower." We become the flower, we wander through the molecular structure of a flower. Each time, we get deeper and deeper into actually merging. It's this incredible bubbling-up thing, and we can't shut it up. The soul is the sorcerer's apprentice, the God, the great divine, which is forever ongoing. It never begins, and it never ends. We cannot possibly hold this limitlessness in our finite mind. All we can do is to allow the experience of it to expand, to merge more and more, and as we do that, we feel the center more and more.

That's what's going to happen to our sexual energy. As soon as consciousness opens to ecstatic energy, it falls into matter, because ecstasy sources creation. We remember the frequency of that energy when we can see the center point between the unmanifest and manifest. It's a figure eight. We are just beginning to touch the outer layers of the center point now. At the second we palpate that conception, we create matter. The more we help people to expand their egos, to expand their consciousness, the deeper they will penetrate the center point. The more they are able to pull through that which is unmanifest into manifestation, the more they will get used to the new frequency. As soon as they have a grasp that they have felt an aspect of the inner God force, they immediately can fall into identifying with it.

All destructive behaviors have to do with fear. Again, as we come into body, we tend to shut off our remembrance of our divine selves. Perhaps in some lifetime we have chosen a blueprint that deals with a traumatic and uncomfortable experience, and we know it's coming. We all know it's coming. There's nothing in the future, because time and space are just illusions in the first place. We are all perceiving what's out there and what we are going to draw it in. Then, because of fear, we attempt to crouch behind the veil, to avoid the lessons that are there. It is an emotional-body response to fear.

There are other response patterns. We have master glands in the head, the pineal and pituitary glands, which are part of the endocrine system. On the spiritual level, these master glands radiate huge spans out into the atmosphere, into the cosmic waves of our interconnectedness to each other, into the universe, and perceive and draw in energy and information. They are the antennas which activate telepathic and other higher-consciousness perceptual faculties. The glands are out there perceiving what we might call a nonlinear dimension. Unfortunately, this capacity on the part of the master glands to act as the spiritual threshold within our bodies extracts a terrible toll on the physical body itself. These high frequencies utilized by the glands expend a tremendous amount of energy. It is the shakti (life force) that courses through the chakras and provides the energetic linkup. The shakti in turn siphons copious amounts of blood sugar from the brain to maintain the "exalted" energy level. The pancreas is called into action continually to respond, and invariably, hypoglycemia and other sugar disorders follow. This scenario creates havoc on the physical body level, and the result is that an inordinate percentage of sensitives and psychics are overweight. Even more damaging is the emotional rollercoaster they experience because of blood sugar swings. This is even more exacerbated by the fact that we learn to focus the perceptual gateway at the solar plexus, which is also the pancreatic center of the body. If we could advance our perceptual field to incorporate these complexities of our multiple-body systems, we could engineer a stabilization of energetic integrity, allowing automatic and unfettered expansion of consciousness.

This recognition of energy dynamics is intrinsic to understanding the growing wave of alcoholic addiction around the world today. The quickest way to get sugar into the brain is alcohol. It instantly alters the blood chemistry in the brain. It is very revealing to explore the alcoholic syndrome from this perspective.

One of the things that is almost always characteristic of alcoholics is that they are profoundly sensitive. They have not been as successful at closing the veil, the passage to multi-dimensionality. The judgment and the hate and the anger are too intense in this reality, and they seek to shut it off. Had we viewed them in childhood in terms of spiritual/emotional sensitivity, we might have nipped alcoholism in its physiological bud and helped keep them from retreating into the astral veil. We must learn to perceive children as the multidimensional threshold beings they are and support their innate spirituality as a gift of value and function within our world. Alcoholism is on the rise proportionate to the degree of our unconsciousness and denial of our true multidimensional, spiritual identities.

Sometimes, self-identity precipitates a sense of profound separation or alienation between ourselves and the world around us. This comes from the illusion that if others knew our hearts—who we truly are—that they would not choose us. We must choose ourselves, and by that strength live our lives. To pierce the heart of another is to discover that we are the same. There are no unspiritual people on this planet. Yet, the level of focus is always a matter of choice.

We have been conditioned to believe that events in the world are not personally related to us, that our reality is separate. But everything is related and meaningful. AIDS and radiation are teaching us about the illusion of separation. It comforts us to believe that the world is compartmentalized like our lives, but it is not. What began as isolated incidences now looms worldwide. This is a universal opportunity to break our habitual patterns of fear response and immobilization and move up to the challenge of cooperation and solutions.

If we respond to the AIDS and radiation crises from a spiritual perspective, we will transform the meaning of life on this planet! Let me show you what I mean. First, we search our souls to find the divine teaching behind these realities. We should begin by focusing on AIDS as a message related to issues of spirituality. By doing that, we can perceive that part of the new understanding is that limiting sexual expression only to the lower chakras without access to our spiritual, heart chakra (especially with multiple partners) invites disease. Through our addiction to immediate gratification, we have been avoiding this teaching for eons. Witness syphillis, gonorrhea, herpes, chlamydia, AIDS! AIDS manifests itself with another clear message: not enough integrity of bodily defenses to survive. We can translate this directly to not enough self-love and conscious experience of our divine nature to survive.

However, in terms of universal evolutionary leaps of consciousness, AIDS is a perfect healing tool. From my perspective, we are now passing into the funnel of the highest initiation for transcendence — into the co-creative octaves. When we have mastered the mystery of death, we will be able to participate in the divine plan of the universe. We *are* ready! Throughout history, man has experienced great natural disasters which decimated the population — Atlantis, plague, etc. All of these were quick passages through the channel of death. In contrast, AIDS is a relatively slow unwinding of the life force. If we view and utilize it from a spiritual octave, we might see it more like a birthing process. AIDS allows time to explore its hidden meaning, to come into dialogue with our bodies, to view and release our karma, and to transcend the linearity of the mind. It allows us to expand our consciousness to encompass divine truth, wherein lies all the profound love and compassion which we have denied ourselves in this dimension.

Let us use this profound initiation of death as the passage to our multi-dimensionality. We are *not* merely our bodies. Our light does *not* extinguish when we release ourselves from the physical vehicle. If we learn to focus our consciousness on this passage and practice moving across the bridge — in and out of the body — not only will we lose our fear of death, but we will experience the meaning of *grace*.

In truth, we are not yet in the era of healing. We are still well within the grip of self-created prophecy. In the future, the word "healing" will take on an entirely new meaning. It will not be related to this strange attachment we have to inertia, whereby we attempt to freeze all motions and hold ourselves on one point lest we lose control and expand. Healing must not represent an external focus, like a conduit; it must go deeper. Healing will one day refer to the actual energetic process of transmutation, transformation, transcendence. This will not take place until we have "anchored the sky," as my higher self has dictated to me. This means that we must bring the soul within the reality of our earthly body. Then we will raise the dead and know choice, and it will happen soon.

I implore those who have already contracted AIDS in this early phase of its presence on Earth to become the leaders in the search for its resolution on spiritual octaves and transcend what began in darkness to a global gift of enlightened spiritual awareness—a profound teaching to transform our lives. AIDS will give us this teaching, and, in the end, we will dispense with death altogether. Since the advent of understanding of the DNA, we have scientifically held most of the pieces of the life and death puzzle, but we have not been ready spiritually for the responsibility. The hologram is awaiting our awakening. We are almost there!

We as a global soul group must acknowledge this Earth as our home now and bring it along with us on our evolutionary journey. Our refusal to acknowledge the depth of our destructive misuse and disregard for the body of our sacred Earth may well jeopardize our own future. As AIDS is to our human body initiation, so radiation will become to our Earth body. Since we are ignoring the Earth's warning signals, our own bodies are the first to issue forth the danger signs. Over parts of the Earth where radiation is most prevalent, we are beginning to experience its power in our physical bodies—people treated for radiation maladies, skin cancer, male sterility, etc., etc. It matters not whether the source of radiation is from improper disposal, nuclear mishaps, or ozone depletion in the atmosphere—there are no innocent parties, no "them and us," no untouchables—the initiation is about expanding the perceptual field so that we can witness the divine purpose in what is so seemingly adverse to us.

Radiation is light. We are in the evolutionary process of becoming light bodies. Our spiritual nature is of light. If we can recognize the relationship, we can incorporate this energy into our own natures and quicken our frequencies until we fulfill our destinies and become true beings of light. We must embrace this reality as a gift. It is like a new instrument which we have not yet learned to play. The technology of our linear, finite brains does not have the capacity to rid us of radiation, because we are dealing with a boogie man who has a lifetime of 50,000 years. One word describes our choice—*adapt*. If we learn to expand our perceptual field to identify the frequency of radiation, then we can do exactly what we do to perceive the higher self, i.e., quicken our own frequency to match and simply commune with these particles of light force.

It is our unconsciousness and our resistance that create the danger. As we learn to palpate the energetics of radiation, we can strengthen our access to the point of conception. By divine intentionality, we can also demanifest radiation back through the threshold of the formless. Just as that beautiful Hopi manifested the rain, we can all call upon those same universal laws to create a beautiful world for ourselves. But we must start by living the beauty radiating within us.

The body is a vehicle for truth in this dimension. The body never lies. The body is always echoing what's happening in the spirit. I remember a rabbi one time saying, "In the spirit, in the body." I find that to be exactly true. The body is just mirroring those experiences, those recognitions that are already there. Instead of saying, "I'm not pure if I have some disease," embrace that disease from a level of not resisting, and explore for yourself what it's about. Past-life work helps tremendously. Whether it gets rid of the disease or doesn't get rid of it, you're going to come across an understanding which is often in itself enough to allow the mind to clear it.

Often I see people who have had a lot of power and who feel guilty about misusing that power. They will precipitate themselves into this same dimension, lifetime after lifetime, with levels of fears, denial, and "I-can't-ism," saying, "Oh, I can't do it because of . . ." The energy will manifest as a handicap. We need to understand that we only do that for the purpose of growth; that's the only reason we do it. If we don't have eyes, we have ears, or sometimes what we feel or touch is much more valuable to us. Maybe we're not utilizing a part of ourselves because we don't need it. It's always the perspective of the soul, the higher self, not punishing us but giving us something else on which to focus. If we have disabilities, whether physical or mental, we must honor the undeniable truth that it is a teaching tool.

Consciousness pervades everything. There is nothing secret in the universe. What anyone else has ever experienced or known is available to us all. There are some who have learned to utilize this truth and expand their consciousness out into the ethers to contact either extensions of their own cosmic consciousness or other entities who might share their expanded awareness or perceptual view with humanity.

These are the "channels" people have begun to seek out in these times. It can be deeply comforting to sit in the presence of someone who is channeling a spirit that recognizes you and can confirm your inner thoughts, a spirit that can explain the karma of some event in your life or help you converse with someone you love who has died. Sometimes just the sense of unconditional love which comes from these spirits can help us to get our grounding and to go on with our lives. This is a wonderful symbiotic relationship, in that these entities need to be in contact with us as much as we need them. They have chosen to continue their focus on this plane to further the growth of their own souls relative to the lessons of this reality.

We must realize that the laws of energetics are in play here. Being given a piece of information that seems to explain or fit into your own personal karmic puzzle in no way releases you from it or alters your blueprint. Just like psychological understanding, knowing something may ease the pain or help alter behavior patterns, but in and of itself knowing has little effect on the deeper levels of your being. That is why it is so important that the knowing and experience come directly from within yourself. Our work is to attune people to the energetics of these patternings and teach them to become aware of how to remove them from the auric field. It is this energetic transcendence that allows us to become light, radiant beings. Intellectual understanding cannot bring these results. The moment you ask for guidance, you must realize that you are abdicating your choices to someone who is still bound to filter truth through the veil of his or her own crystallized experiences. These entities are energies which still contain a level of positionality, still have a personality level or memory circuit which is focused by the particular patterning of their own understanding.

Even the higher masters, such as Jesus the Christ and others, have some remaining karma on this octave which allows them to maintain channels of communication with us. As their presence expands our conscious awareness of other dimensions, we must help release their souls' bondage to this plane so that they, too, can evolve and extend universal, divine light.

The clearing work of the Institute lends itself beautifully to helping those disincarnate beings release emotional imprints which are entrapping them. It is also exceedingly important to help the channels themselves clear. The degree to which channels are still holding imprints is the degree to which they color or distort information passing through them to someone seeking advice. Psychic accuracy is not significantly hampered by this, because "reading" someone is more a function of tuning in that spiritual enlightenment, per se. Asking someone outside ourselves to sculpt our karmic choices is always risky business.

One common theme among channels is the terrible experience of being punished or put to death for communicating a truth which is out of range for the populace. The body records these memories and guards itself so that the situation never be repeated. The echo of this alarm system spreads out along our illusionary continuum of time and space. We never forget. Once the soul has garnered enough wisdom to function from these heightened octaves of awareness, there will always be an energetic aspect of the system which naturally gravitates towards flowing within those pathways. It is the exquisite higher self connecting up the cosmic waves from which all knowing is accessed. The person tunes into this frequency with the unconscious protective guard in place and thus receives the knowing as if from outside the self. As we release beings from the stick-em of astral memories, channels often discover that it is their higher selves which have been guiding all along. This revelation is a very profound experience for them. There is a tremendous upshifting of energy levels and guidance capacity, and the clarity of their channeling greatly increases as well.

Inner guides are a part of our multidimensional resources as well. Each guide has a frame of reference which relates to our inner development and corresponds to its own level of expertise. One of the troubles we have is becoming addicted to our guides. First we become addicted to our mothers, then to our lovers, then to our children, and we never let go. We get so sticky-fingered that we never let go. Even after we die, we never let go. We become habitual with our guides. If you let this process work the way it's supposed to work, a guide will come in and say, "Over there," and you go over there. Then that guide will go away—unless you hold that guide in bondage—and a new guide will come in. Guides come to pull and twist us. Do your work with them and let them go. Don't always be calling the same guide in, or you're just going to be making bigger circles on a horizontal plane. That's how we grow. We come up to a horizontal plane, and we spread out. When we have that mastery, we make a vertical leap to another horizontal plane, and we spread out again, just like DNA.

It's very important to exercise your capacity to not be attached to some guide with a repertoire related to your own. If you ask a question which is not in its expertise, you're going to get into trouble. It's going to give you a thought-form that's not appropriate to where you really need to be. There are many levels of guides, entities, energies, and beings in every octave of the universe. There are those who are lords, just like there were Grecian gods on one octave of reality, and ascended masters on another octave of reality. There are lords of the universe, the galactic frequencies. They are all there to pick and choose from in relation to your own attraction/repulsion mechanisms. They are all orchestrating to bring this planet, which is so desperately out of balance, into balance.

Your higher self issued forth from you, and it will be bright enough and strong enough to put you in connection with anyone you want out there. But as lords of the universe, it is not their command that we should do this or we should do that.

You must experience the light that you can create yourself. As you experience the light, your focus will be on using that light. Then you can harmonize with the various ascended masters or the lords of the universe or galactic beings or Christic energy or any of those. They are not separate. They are all just different factors of reality, like the higher self. There is something for everybody, just like the plant, mineral, and animal kingdoms. Whatever your patterning is, there's somebody or something out there who will respond. It's best to become as universal as possible yourself, to extend your own repertoire.

There is no comparison between guides of any nature and the higher self. There is no channel like your own higher self. It is the energy of your divine being. The higher self is the best guide because it is not attached to any human perspective. The higher self is the *only* energy which can access your personal hologram in and of itself as it interfaces with the infinite, divine cosmos. Exploration outside the self may have as much to do with learning levels of discernment as it does with truth. The higher self is always within the realm of truth, always intrinsic to our experience of consciousness. The higher self is always taking us "home."

◇

◇SIX◇
ASTRAL
ENERGETICS

*As we spin up the
spiral vortex of life,
all dimensional realities
can move to that quickening
evolutionary process
along with us.*

At The Light Institute, sessions are a journey into suspended time, when we go deep within for the symbols, the images, and the colors. These are the language of the unconscious.

As we journey within consciousness during sessions, one of the most difficult concepts to grasp is that of the astral energy in the emotional body. We have an astral body which is composed of our own emotions, our own auric field. What does the astral body look like? It is a body that looks just like the physical body but extends out from it. It is the astral body that lifts up from the physical vehicle when we go out of body, and it moves through the astral dimensions, sometimes through octaves of infrared.

Our auric field is composed of a coalesced emotional or astral body, which moves from our physical vehicle out through that cord connecting the physical and astral body and into the astral dimension. The difficulty arises when strong emotional imprints radiate out like antennas, drawing to us imprints from those astral dimensions. We come back from the astral experience and perhaps spend days clearing our auric field without any true understanding of what it is all about. People commonly go out of body during sleep, accidents, trauma, or surgery. Just think of the consequences of going out of body during surgery when the hospital is filled with the entities that have just died and all the fear and sorrow that accompanies them. In the unprotected astral state, we are totally permeable to these extraneous emotions.

If we begin to look at our emotional bodies in that perspective, we can see that so much of that which jerks us around, which controls our perspective of reality—how we feel about ourselves and the world—is not even really ours. It is just us amplifying, magnifying emotions that could or should be only a flicker, that would otherwise just pass through us. It is the old mob psychology. There is a profound alteration in the individual's centering when that person gets in a crowd, a drunken state, or in the astral dimension. Generally, crowds function from the astral dimension. That is why they get involved in things that individuals could never do by themselves.

The emotional body is imprinted with astral energy, which is very seductive in nature. We call it "stick-em." The astral dimension is in simultaneous space with this dimension. Emotions, shock, drugs, and dreams are all mechanisms which trigger breaking through the envelope into the astral.

Delving into past lives always takes us into the astral as well. The second we come into form, we are contacting our astral energy. The astral dimension is the veil; it is part and parcel of the emotional body, whose imprint follows us from lifetime to lifetime. This energy actually exists in the body cells, and each time we are reborn, it reactivates itself within cellular memory. Because of that, the emotional body takes up its old place, harboring its old stuff. It sets up a frequency through its astral energy that radiates out to the physical vehicle, which sets up the message that allows reality. The emotional body is controlling the show because of its astral nature.

It is important to see that the astral energy flows into the cells of the body. The cells have the physicality that allows them to access whatever the emotional body has experiencd within its timeless labyrinth. The emotional body carries through those messages—memories of fear, of destruction, of disaster, and rarely memories of ecstasy. The emotional body separates from the unmanifest and does not merge back in. Ecstasy does not filter through simply because we have not evolved an emotional repertoire of a high enough vibration to include rapture, bliss, ecstasy. These are experienced by the light body.

As long as judgment and self-righteousness cannot make contact with direct experience, we are caught on this side of the veil, the physical side, and are separated from the God-source. Once we are willing to move into the astral and work with the stick-em, move into memories of all those lifetimes of experiences and release them, we are peeling away the veil that allows us to return to pure form. As long as we allow the stick-em to dominate, we can reach for the God-source, we can talk about it, think about it, and conceptualize it somewhat in the body, but we cannot *experience* it because the emotional body is the vehicle of experience.

We do not see the astral dimension at first, because if we saw it, all we would see is pain and anger, guilt and contortion. Since we are still attached to these experiences, we avoid them. Because the astral memory is cellular, we must clear ourselves at the cellular level. And that is why, in this state of evolution, we have come to a stalemate, because the mental body can no longer protect us. It must expand now; we must move the finite mind outside of this treadmill groove and into a holographic patterning which will allow it to identify for us those other octaves which are real—ecstasy and rapture, the frequency of our divine nature. In the presence of these energies, the physical and emotional bodies are spontaneously transformed.

If we are inadvertantly triggered into the astral dimension, we are defenseless to the onslaught of emotional energies. Those energies, which may derive from particular thought-forms or ancient emotions, are often of a very low vibratory level. They impinge on our defenseless consciousness and infiltrate our experience of ourselves. They are like parasites that attach themselves to our being. After we come back from the astral dimension, they continue to activate and grow, disturbing the integrity of our being. This is why we often find ourselves engaged in feelings which are basically foreign to ourselves, such as a sudden anxiety which has no evident source. The feeling is encapsulated in the energy carried back across the veil to infiltrate us in this dimension.

The lack of center core in the astral dimension allows emotional energies to be absorbed without discrimination. This lack of ego center is part of the intrigue of drugs from a psychological or emotional perspective. When people utilize recreational drugs to relax, they are able to loosen the fabric of their egos so they are less defensive, less hostile, less anxious. But the price of that loosening of the ego, as it takes us into astral reality, is that we have no center of our self-awareness. We become lost in an endless sea of erratic energies which attach themselves to us. Of course, it is often our ulterior motive to escape our daily lives, to escape our egos, which are the confines of our self-limitation. So we venture into the astral. Not only do we escape our ego in the astral, but a schism is created between our various realities and our capacities to move along those realities in a fluid, conscious way. This is a disruption of our life purpose.

The physiological confirmation of that disruption is quite fascinating. It has been found, for example, that most drugs create an imprint within the iris of the eye that is present up to fifteen years after those experiences. Marijuana produces a tar-like sticky substance which coats the synapse of nerve pathways within the brain, and to this date we have not discovered a technology capable of removing that residue. This blockage diminishes our freedom of expanded consciousness by slowing down our vibration. The astral dimension vibrates within very low frequency ranges.

The spiritual teachings of many native cultures have incorporated the use of substances specifically for the purpose of triggering consciousness into the astral dimension. This was so that guidance and union could be made with the consciousness of other species, of other realms, through which these seekers could ascertain information important to survival, to understanding the future, and to daily life. In zoomorphic patternings which have been prevalent in the Americas, plant substances were utilized to contact and merge with the astral spirit of animals. The power of such animals was seen to relate directly to the quality of human lives, as well as to be accessible to guide humans within the holograms of all species, of all nature living in harmony. The intercommunication within the dimensions and the species within that natural construct was of a divine purpose. It was always part of those rituals, those substances or those identifications with the spirits of animals, to lose the self. The goal was to lose the constriction of the ego in order to understand, communicate, and channel a higher energy, the energy of the Great Spirit. In this way, the communication with the astral dimension was a guide to the native person. But the intentionality of purpose and the focus was always very directed. Those beings who participated in the moving back and forth to bring the gift were not asked to do more than that sacred sacrifice for their people. The power of understanding was not stressed in the everyday life within any community of beings.

86

At this point in history, it is a very difficult procedure to maneuver ourselves back and forth across the astral veil without becoming a polluted medium of those energies prevalent in the astral dimension. At the present time, because of scientific experimentation with laser beams, the actual membrane between the dimensions has been ripped open. There are particular places on the planet where the astral energy bleeds out. People who indulge in hallucinatory drugs, even very casually, or allow themselves to lose ego-control through other means—through alcohol, or stressed emotional experiences—find themselves contending with these runaway energies from the astral dimension which are causing tremendous pollution on a psychic, emotional, and mental level. When there is clear definition and mastership with regard to the astral dimension, then we can use it to guide us, to help to educate us as to what is going on in this world. But outside the confines of that mastership, it is very destructive to participate in the erratic energetics of the astral dimension on an individual level, because it creates separation between ourselves and others, between ourselves and our own higher consciousness.

We cannot connect in a coalesced, focused, centered way when we are inundated with astral energy. We lose our identity and our purpose without the integration present in traditional peoples who have organized themselves around those specific, sacred tasks. At the same time, it is my profound experience of truth that we must now release ourselves from all our past memories of participation in rituals with substances which have placed us in the astral dimension. We desperately need to advance the octaves of our conscious capacity within higher realms, from which we can glean more wisdom as to the essential purpose of our lives beyond personal power.

We must move beyond the power of the astral dimension to manipulate, through alchemy of whatever kind, the realities around us. Instead, we must now hear the whispering of a higher order, wherein we can release our history so that we participate in this dimension as fully realized beings. This allows our life purpose to move from personal power to universal flow, to communion on a universal level, so that our thought-forms and our energy become global in nature. We need no longer create from the limitations of our individual will, which does not cognate the hologram, the interconnection between the trillions of threads which are orchestrated into the fabric of a harmonious tapestry of life. When, through our subtle memory, we are induced to go back into rituals which have served us at other times and other lifetimes with some level of personal mastery, power, or information, we are picking up the thread of the consciousness which created those rituals to access that particular octave of reality. That consciousness was appropriate within the hologram of its reality in time, but it is not necessarily appropriate, complete, or sufficient to provide us with enlightenment or survival at this time.

We must understand that the ritual and the consciousness are married to the appropriate experience of souls incarnated within those reality zones. We must not repeat our history ourselves; history must now move along the evolutionary continuum of expansion in order to utilize faster, higher, more appropriate octaves of enlightenment which answer to the reality of the situation we have incarnated into at this time. Our past will not serve us here. It is not because the wisdom was impure or incomplete then, but because the utilization—the medium of that wisdom within the consciousness of those times—does not meet our present needs. The universe is not static; it is always evolving.

If we allow ourselves to let go of that history impregnated in our astral emotional bodies, we can then access our multidimensionality, which includes higher octaves. Releasing that frequency of the past produces the propulsion into the finer, faster frequencies of understanding that would serve us now. We must explore other worlds!

It is important to understand that, like the energy of infrared, all material substances are impregnated with the frequency of experience—stored in the astral dimension. Places where we have participated in experiences which have emotional qualities, intensities, and energies seem to have those frequencies encapsulated within that area over time. This is true even of inanimate objects. Furniture in our homes is impregnated with the quality of emotional contact to which it has been exposed. If you end a relationship—let us say a twenty-year marriage—and you take your furniture to a new place, that furniture is radiating the emotions of previous experiences. The consequence is that you are still entrapped and constantly stimulated unconsciously (astrally) by the emotional quality of your experiences. All matter radiates this "astral smoke," and this affects how we perceive ourselves, how we feel, and how we behave emotionally, even though we have forgotten the source of the emotions.

Let me give you an example. Perhaps you go with your mate to a wonderful, romantic place and stay in a Victorian hotel. You sit on the Victorian chairs and sleep in the Victorian bed. You muse at all the attention to form that was a part of Victorian times, the ornate design. You came for a romantic interchange, yet the energy radiating from the consciousness which created these ornate particles of matter once addressed itself to the belief that sexual activity is dry, duty-bound, unpleasant, or forbidden. The time comes to experience a wonderful lovemaking, and, for no reason understandable to your consciousness, you are suddenly repulsed by your partner. The withdrawal, the change of mood, the sense of isolation or even forboding is because the living, physical antenna of your body is receiving thought-forms, messages, and experiences from these physical entities such as chairs, rooms, and places.

It is magnificent to begin to recognize these truths. From the beginning of time, sensitives have understood these principles, these laws of energy. By even placing a hand on an object, we can access the quality of knowing, of experience, of emotions, which are related to those physical objects—a chair, a piece of jewelry, a piece of ground, or someone's body.

The astral, because it is not in time and in space, is a great repository of emotional history. While some of this information can be useful to us, most of it is not. We need to be new beings of a higher frequency.

It is not just touch that allows us to recognize or cognate information from astral fields. Even through our visual sense, we can perceive astral emanations. There are astral emanations which radiate out from the television, out from the things we see around us in the physical world. The psychology of media is well versed in this understanding, so that commercials on television are directed to this unconscious cueing. The media stimulates unconscious desires within us so that we will respond in a way someone else wishes. It influences our buying, molds our opinions and our choices in daily life. It is a profound, astral pollution that is forced upon us as we passively watch television. We are so enamored by our intellectual minds as we watch some program that we are not aware that we are infiltrating ourselves with its judgment. We define and create the fabric of our own positionality by allowing ourselves to be impregnanted with sounds, images, and suggestions from all the media around us.

What we see in terms of sexual innuendos in the media affects us profoundly, because it allows us to seed within the mind visual-mental fantasies which carry us into the astral, illusionary worlds. Our physical, real contact with our sexual nature is blocked from meaningful experience by these astral infiltrations. The biochemical, subtle electrical changes in the brain from mental stimulation are often more real to us than the actual physical experience. This has been very destructive to relationships and to our sexual nature because the profound electromagnetic energy which is released is a great threshold into the astral dimension.

Past-life work shows us over and over again that sexual preferences, sexual experiences in past lives, are indelibly laid down within the coding of subsequent bodies, both emotional and physical. When we abuse the sacredness of our sexual energy through promiscuity, we take within our being the astral energy of not only our lover but all the partners of our lover! This is being brought home to us with the truth of AIDS and other diseases related to sexual communication. One of the messages of AIDS is that there's not enough self-coalition to do the simple process of defending the body. When we have three or four other bodies entering into our auric field, we lose our integrity; our impermeable encapsulation of self gets knocked out. This is exactly why so many people experience exhaustion after making love.

Sexual energy should create tremendous energy within the vehicle, not consume or exhaust it. If, then, any kind of engagement creates that disassociation, that decrystallization of the center of a being, then it is inviting disease. Lovemaking causes the auric fields to mix and stay joined for about forty-eight hours. The quality of emotions, thought-forms, and other astral energy in our partner's auric field can move without restriction into our own field. Even a short affair takes about nine months to clear. If you are not vibrating on similar octaves, as is the case in chance encounters, a palpable wobble in your being is most likely to occur. This is not a scenario of the heart. Because the energy is linked in the lower chakras, there is a jamming of the pelvic energy. It is a rare woman who does not exhibit this phenomenon, whether the result is due to abortion, guilt, or inability to experience her own body.

The '60s opened the passageway to the search for real sexual response. But women responded all too often by barricading themselves behind vaginal walls. Cervical cancer and other pelvic-inflammatory diseases have followed with alarming regularity. Merging in the genital area is the closest we've come to merging in our limited consciousness. We can really feel ourselves when we get an electrical jolt in the sexual area. It is probably the most intensity that people feel in themselves. It is our closest experience of ecstasy. Now we must awaken our sexual energy to the *next* level, so that we can begin to recognize and assimilate body energetics and universal, cosmic frequencies. In truth, we already intrinsically know who carries an energy which nourishes us and who doesn't. It's just that the sticky astral energy of karma is too seductive to resist, and so we fall into the same trap over and over, often with the same accomplices we've utilized in other lifetimes, other experiences. All the diseases which produce aging and death will be gone when we access the wisdom of the higher self. We will begin to have a focus which understands completion, the totality of the sexual energy—with or without another person. Thus we can lift our frequency into that cosmic, orgasmic state which does not include separation.

Alcoholism can be seen in the auric field. Alcoholism is a disease. It's not a matter of lack of will or being too sensitive to survive, although that is sometimes a part of it. One of the ways to help an alcoholic is to check the levels of hypoglycemia and correct the imbalance, because it is almost always there. Interestingly enough, it's there almost 100% of the time for psychics, who have big problems with invasion of their auric field. That whole syndrome of imbalance in the blood-sugar level tends to make psychics fairly heavy. It's because the pituitary and pineal glands are out there receiving information instead of paying attention to the body. Instead of saying, "OK, thyroid, pump away," and "OK, endrocrine system, move," they're out there and just don't focus on the body.

For alcoholics, one way to help them is to work with the hidden hypoglycemia which is there. L-glutamine, an amino acid, helps people stop wanting to drink by balancing the blood-sugar level in the brain. So, for people who do a lot of drinking each day, or for people who have alcoholic tendencies, they can take L-glutamine in the late morning and late afternoon. It's one of the few substances that passes the membrane into the brain and stabilizes the the blood sugar. It smooths out the nervousness so that emotional upheavals are not so extreme.

L-glutamine is wonderful for all of us to smooth out the roller-coastering that goes on as we move in and out of dimensions. One of the things that happens as we expand our consciousness is that we all have some kind of difficulty staying with the body or utilizing the body. It is very important to be in this body for each and every one of us, to find a way to unconditionally learn to love this vehicle, to use it as the honing for ourselves, as the instrument of the unmanifest in this dimension. Every cell in the body has recorded that moment of conception, of manifesting the unmanifest, and we must begin to focus differently on the body

Our auric fields are very important in terms of the palpability of astral energy. Once we are able to identify the auric field, we can use it to monitor astral pollution and clear ourselves of unwanted energy. As our consciousness expands to include recognition of auric fields, we can utilize them as barometers of truth, to truly know ourselves and each other. The aura is its own truth. It never lies, not in this lifetime, not in any lifetime. It tells the story of who we really are; it is the physical akashic record, accessible through the cellular mind.

The aura is simply an electromagnetic field that radiates from the body. It is constantly changing; we don't have green auras and we don't have blue auras. We have auras that are pulsating all the time and constantly changing. They change with our every thought. They change with our every feeling. They have certain perspectives or personalities just like we do, just like our bodies have certain messages. Auras are the same way. They send out messages in relationship to that karma we have chosen. Thus we may have an aura that has a lot of one positionality, with a lot of blue, a lot of orange, a lot of green, according to the blueprint of our soul's design.

We do palpate each other's auras. There's no question about that. We like people or we don't like them, and the thing that we like or dislike is what we feel in their auric fields. If we feel fear or anger in the auric field, we will likely withdraw from them. If we could see it, we would see a color in relationship to that.

I have the great fortune of knowing a woman who is one of the world's masters on auric fields. She was gifted with the capacity from birth to see the chakric spinning. Let me very briefly share with you what she has taught me, as she is an exquisite master. Each chakra has all the colors in it—even the crown chakra mixes all those colors because the energies are all intertwining as they come up to the crown. However, as each color carries a frequency specific to certain energetics, these energetics will prevail in the chakra which corresponds directly to them.

If you're looking at the solar plexus chakra, for example, you may see more green, because green is the actual vibration of the emotional body. But if you could see the chakra spinning, what you would see is multitudinous fibers of all the colors that extend out. Along the fibers of each color are little conglomerates. In eastern traditions, they call them *nadis*. Nadis may be within the body, within the auric field, or within the nervous system. They look like little globs of seaweed along ropes. If you could take some kind of machine and look at your auric field in that way, that's what it actually looks like—in its fiber form, you would see all the colors coming out.

If something is constricting in some way, it will change the color frequencies. If your heart is constricting, your blues in the heart chakra will pull in; the fibers will be short. They'll wrap around each other, or they'll wrap around the mother fiber or the lover fiber, or whatever is telling the story, whatever is constricting or blocking the energy of that chakra. We now have machines that test the auric field and can show if it's out or in or broken.

Drugs have been a great tool of learning for us in terms of our extended perception of subtle body-fields. Once you have, under any circumstances, popped out of your third-dimensional self into a place where you're seeing rainbow-colored energies radiating out from people, plants, everything you see, you never quite recover from it. An expansion has taken place. However, there's a price that's paid, and if you do it with drugs, your auric field is scarred. Drugs put a hole in it. It's like cutting into the body and creating an incision, the scar of which rarely goes away. It gets better, but it disrupts the integrity of the field of the energy that you have radiating out from you. Inharmonious sex, drugs, and alcohol weaken our force fields to the extent that they literally wilt and sometimes may even leak! This is why we lose sight of our goals and feel powerless to exert ourselves. Our life force is draining away from us, leaving depression and dismay to rule our sense of purpose and participation.

If, when we experience this inertia, we could palpate our chakras and auric fields, we could use our conscious, loving intention to clear and strengthen the aura. The best way to do this is by extending the light energy out through the solar plexus so that our force field flows out around us. Stretching out the aura in this way actually clears the emotional body and provides us natural protection from astral energy because, as the tide of energy moves out, no energy can flow in against it.

It is not that we should view the astral dimension as a negative experience to be avoided. But, we should understand the nature of the astral so that we can utilize it with clarity and consciousness about how we interact with energy. Then we can garner the wisdom and the access of intercommunication between interspecies and interdimensions that would be useful in our daily lives. At the same time, as we release our own astral energy to consciousness, we are healing, recreating, and altering the astral dimension itself. As we spin up the spiral vortex of life, all dimensional realities can move to that quickening evolutionary process along with us. We are dancing across the membrane of these dimensions, across the expanse of the universe within divine grace.

◇

SEVEN

SEXUALITY

Sexuality is not what separates us from enlightenment; sexuality is an inherent quality of our Earth experience which merges us into enlightenment.

It was an odyssey we had made before. Always at Christmas, my inner core seemed to become strangely restless and agitated by the externalization of some deep energy within me. Once the "floor-plan" of a family is irrevocably disturbed by the finality of divorce, family occasions such as Christmas no longer ring true because they are markers on a historic continuum. A hole in the family fabric inevitably breaks that continuum. We created a new marker by going down to the gentle desert around Tucson at Christmas. I felt whole and happy with my five children surrounding me—sleeping, eating, exploring together in an environment without superficial distraction.

It seemed perfect to sleep out under the stars on Christmas Eve. The beauty, the newness, the vulnerability of it sparked my unquenchable emotion which soared up into the night sky. The expansion stirred my body which considered the difference between pressing my heart up against another heart, and this open-ended rushing. It had been four months since I had made love and I mused about hte serious possibility that I would never experience those sensations again. I was forty-one, my sexual energy honed to its sweetest, highest pitch. I laughed to myself at the thought that what I had experienced in the last several years made me feel bursting, as if I alone had made a new discovery which would change the world. Here I was, fresh with this new "stuff," and now I was never to revisit its secret world.

I don't know how long I slept, but I awakened to a trillion orgasmic explosions, pulsating electrical spasms shattering the confines of my cells, my body, my consciousness!

I was streaming. All borders, all awareness of where I began and ended was gone. After indescribable, timeless moments, it quieted into a sensation of an undulating sea and I realized that I had literally levitated more than a foot above the ground. I felt a sensation of floating down, and for the rest of the night I listened to a wonderful humming within my body. My cells were singing. My mind never stirred itself throughout, I was so engulfed in the experience. Only now could I give it a name: I call it "cosmic orgasm."

The spiritual essence of sexuality is the unmanifest, multidimensional force of creation flowing into thought which descends into matter. It is our experience of that which is unmanifest, the created and ever-spiraling enclosed loop of nothingness. Life-force energy descends to the thought level, and at the level of thought, there is a vibrational effect that begins to undulate within the creative force far out across the universe. That undulation begins to form itself in structure, in rhythm. It creates materiality, and that materiality begins to seek its own level, begins to seek its home so that the seed is birthed within the environment that creates life.

That moment when the energy connects is the moment we call conception. Conception takes place on several octaves, several dimensions. Conception is the midpoint for us between the unmanifest and the manifest. This joining creates a fission that echoes out, creating a universe, creating an environment that then allows that which is within to grow. There is a synchronicity: that which is to grow and that which creates.

In our human dimension there is that flow, that fission—when the egg and the sperm unite—and it creates the experience which radiates out an imprint or a pattern that defines the form, and expresses the intentionality of the soul. As a new being begins to grow, it holds within itself that whisper of the intentionality of the soul.

At the moment of conception, the frequency is already set in motion that upon maturation will draw to us our partners. Those beings who come to us for sexual connection are within the scope of that vibration, within the scope of that frequency at the moment of conception. All the cells of the body mature into the years and continue that growth or that life-pulse until the point of puberty.

The energy of the pineal gland is directly related to the material form which represents that conception, nourishes that form, and which holds the imprint. The pineal gland becomes stimulated so that the unmanifest, which is spirit, funnels in on that which takes form, such as in the sexual, genital area.

It is very important to understand this sexual connection, because when the spiritual energy and the body imprint an octave of separation or duality, then the pineal gland very often does not attend to the physicality of the body; instead, the sexual energy is disturbed or does not follow the flow that would take it into what we call normal sexual manifestation. Thus, sexual energy stays out of physicality, so that creation comes in from other octaves of our bodies—our mental bodies, our essence frequencies—and does not come fully into the physical vehicle.

In the structure of the genital organs, there lies the essence of that calling: the energy which radiates out, attracts the energy of those partners, and produces the growth or the choices that the genital area is to experience. When these memories are dislodged—when the imprint is filled with experiences whose densities reflect on disease or death of those areas—they create blockage in the present vehicle, a separation of the flow from the lower chakras to the higher chakras. This is what we are experiencing now, from the experimentation on sexuality that has gone on since Atlantis through medieval times to the present. That experience is activating the physical structures, and we have much abnormality, wherein the spiritual essence which should be present within the genital organs is blocked. Women, for example, continue to search for some echo of that fission that took place, and instead, experience a deadening of the walls of the vagina which does not allow the electromagnetic frequency to take place. The natural orgasmic creative state is experienced only in its primitive form, rather than in its fullness. The same is true with the yang force that is striking outward because of its memory imprint. Sexual union is not allowed to come full circle between the juices which extend outward and the juices being created to draw back in, and so we have blockage.

When the physical body is unable to experience the hologram, the flowing out and flowing in, there is a profound agitation that takes place, because it does not reach the point of conception, the threshold. When we understand this, and when we tune our consciousness back across the line from physicality, back through the essence of electromagnetic energy, back to the source, we then can bring that energy out of its isolation and back up through the entire vehicle, or physical body.

The vehicle is the representation of the God force from the pineal gland through the genitals, back up through the system, to create the figure eight, the whole. This is the divine circuitry. We can then begin to access the energy as it was meant to be, so that it flows out through all the chakric systems; the chakras represent those passages, those octaves and levels of growth in consciousness, which allow the divine play. We, through the vehicle, through the sexual energy, can then transmute ourselves from that which is totally within the realm of form to that which is totally outside the realm of form, by allowing the thread of consciousness, which is the initial flow, to move. We can use that energy within any of the octaves of creation which we are being called upon to use at this time.

We must teach ourselves to access those octaves of our sexual energy so that we produce a whole within ourselves, so that we radiate the energy out. Then all beings we touch or come into contact with can have that stimulation of memory, that directing magnetic energy that allows them to begin to flow through the meshwork of their own octave, so that they attract energies which are similar to their own. Thus we can free people from the confusion of scattering sexual energy, which causes disease and separation rather than that merging which is the essence of life.

We must begin to pull that energy up through our system and see where it stops, so that we can clear the octave of the residue that blocks it from coming back in the physical form to the pineal gland and returning to the beginning. By putting sexual frequency into this environment, we bring about cohesiveness, a creative force that has not yet been here on this planet. It is this creative force that can assist the human form with its destiny, its will to be, which will erase the confusion and disease. We have always associated the word "sexuality" with genital activity. As we broaden our experience of it as shakti, divine life force, we will use it to heal, to create. As we embrace it within ourselves, shame and seduction will surrender to joy and freedom.

We need to look at this in terms of that choice of a partner, that person who creates the dance with us on a physical octave. We need to experience the energy, the sexual energy in its essential form, so that when we are making love we stay in contact on that octave. What happens when we do this is we lose our positionality. We lose the separation between the male and the female, that aspect which penetrates and that aspect which receives. Because each being, whether in a physical male or female body, has both of these. Until we are released into balance, conception, and merging, we cannot be truly balanced in any octave of ourselves. When we can let go of the sensation of the body which is positioned in either the penetration or the receiving, we can begin to experience the energetics in a profoundly different way. We can begin to focus our energy to experience the fluidity of the electric impulse. When the vagina has awakened, it will flow. The same with the male organ. There is that liquid form that carries the electrical energy, that pulsates. It is a consciousness that can move into that octave of exchange. Again, the positionality is lost, and what happens is conception, the point of creation. When we learn to access that energy in such a pure form, we can then use the energy of conception to create rain, or food, or abundance of any kind. Likewise, we can move to the other side and release negativity, demanifest atomic waste or any pollution of energy which does not serve ourselves or the planet.

The male, then, can pull from the female her fluids, as well as extend fluids to the female who can receive. When that happens, the energy will come together, and each being will be able to facilitate it up through the chakric system without effort, and all of the centers of communication, of merging, of reality, are opened.

When you contact creative force in all dimensions, then you do not need the closure of that creative force, just as you do not need to close the auric field for protection. It is not sexuality which separates us from enlightenment; sexuality is an inherent quality of our Earth experience which merges us with enlightenment. It is that which allows us to rush forward and become the divine. The body was not designed to be separate from God. It was only our incapacity to hold, to experience the hologram that created the separation. When we begin to push through that—and that is why we are having sexual confusion and sexual disease at this time— and recognize that God, the divine force, is within all, we can then use sexuality as a tool. Our sexual energy is the closest energy to spirit. It is the closest energy to the divine force, because conception is that point where the unmanifest takes form, where the merging takes place and pulsation begins. The pulsation begins, and the life force radiates out and creates form. Form is the extension of God. Form is the extension of the divine. The divine reaches out through matter in order to experience itself.

What is happening, then, is for the first time ever, we can begin to consciously use our sexual energy as part of our experience of the divine. That's what I'm saying when I talk about cosmic orgasm, when I talk about rapture, about ecstasy. That is why ecstasy is a new frequency, the vibration of a new octave. Our sexual energy is usually the only place in our life where we come anywhere close to ecstasy or rapture because we feel that pulsation, that electromagnetic charge that is a part of our own creation. It is the essence of our being. We can really feel that ecstasy.

The difficulty that we have had up until now, on this planet in our physical bodies, is that our capacity for conception has only taken place within a very limited scope, in a very limited octave of physical reality. Shall we say, within the first two chakras? We must open the rest of our chakras for conception so that we can merge to the highest octave. The heart chakra will, for the first time, be exposed to that creative energy. This planet is the planet of the heart chakra. When the sexual energy lives within the heart, we will not have disease, we will not have confusion. We will not have issues over where we live, how we are nourished, or how we experience life, because we will live its very essence. Conception is the threshold to multidimensionality.

We must now begin the task of drawing on this sexual energy that has become cumbersome to us, because it has only been used for birthing, dying and manipulation, or mutilation of the physical body. This energy must now find its way into the essential form, into the heart, into an octave which carries materiality and life, so that we can bring the merger together here on Earth. If we can appreciate even the humor of people making love from the heart, then we can begin to merge on these octaves of the creative force. It is the God force that must descend into the physical vehicle so that it can now come through to the death, to the dying octave. Then it can again move on to the ever-radiant octave of life, where the heart is activated, where there is no separation, where there is a true merger. Death can be lost, can fade away, which is the purpose of this time on this planet; it is to move into an octave of participation on a creative level. Sexual energy could be the key.

We have to move from this into the higher frequencies, and each one of us can do this whether or not we have partners. We must do this at this time, or we cannot help the flow of humanity through this difficult period. We must be able to activate this energy as a reality, so that when people come and say, "I'm having confusion," "I have two partners," "I have herpes," we can bring them through so that they can find themselves. It's the same kind of work we've been doing in other octaves, in other ways. Now we must include in our repertoire the recognition and use of sexual energy as it really is. Instead of blocking, we must lift people up so that they can access the energy from higher chakras and use that energy to come back around and clear the disease. People have so overexposed their bodies for sexual gratification that they have surrendered their natural, protective impermeability. This has resulted in AIDS and the sexual diseases which are challenging us now.

The greatest weapon, the greatest laser to alter any disease, blockage, numbness, or death within the physical structure of our sexuality is our access to the force of creation. This God force can be palpated, astringed, and directed. When people who feel sexual confusion, blockage, or disease can contact the higher essence of sexuality, they will flush the chakras. In flushing the chakras, they will flush the subtle bodies and the physical body, literally working out the emotional, mental, and physical debris.

There is no one who doesn't have to clear sexual blockages, because we have been born to this time when we are here to clear. Who among us does not have our sexual history, our baggage that we bring with us that says, "This is how I identify myself." That baggage has been there simply to give us something to wrap ourselves around. Every one of us can move into those octaves of the heart, so that we can reach what is necessary to clear at this time.

In the same way that we do our work at the Institute, we are here to begin to peel away the layers of that sexual identity, that sexual positionality. What is male? What is female? What is the manifest and unmanifest on any octave? It is the search for these energies that has created so many disruptions in relationships. They are each within us all. We habitually come together out of need because we project the male or female essence as being part of the energy we seek from our partners. Once we have learned to tap it within ourselves, our relationships will go through a complete metamorphosis. The very first cell of our physical form is both male and female. When we can experience that on an energetic level, we can re-shift within every one of our trillions of cells our understanding, our capacity to embrace both of those energies and allow them to merge by loving them.

It isn't that we need to judge or isolate sexual confusion. We can honor sexual confusion just as we honor all of the themes which burn the fuel for enlightenment. As we separate that confusion of who-I-am and who-you-are, all of those themes of ownership, possession, separation, loss, and denial will lose their definition, will lose their form and begin to drop away. They'll drop away in the same way that the emotional body begins to quicken and speed up. All of it will disperse because that's the law—pulsation, universal flow.

Everyone outside us mirrors us. That is why it's so absurd to isolate ourselves behind these mind-concepts of sexuality as heterosexuality, bisexuality, or homosexuality. They don't really exist. On a multidimensional level, we have numerous and varied sexual repertoires. It is the unconscious memory of those repertoires that attracts us into recreating the imprints, even in these bodies which may be vastly different than those bodies—hence the confusion. Let me give you an example from a past-life session.

A being from the planet Saturn volunteered to participate on a mission to planet Earth to help seed a more advanced civilization. On Saturn, sexual procreative activity never includes penetration on physical levels, but instead is produced by mutual thought-form. For the purpose of this mission to Earth, the being exchanged an androgynous body for a male body in order to impregnate the Earth beings with the proposed genetic coding. The horror of actual penetration of another being was so intense for the Saturnian that he joined a homosexual group rather than continue the sexual practices predominant on Earth. Communion with like kind was more tolerable than participating in an unthinkable, interpersonal affront from the perspective of the Saturnian culture at that time. We haven't lifted our physical vehicles to an octave where the mind-concepts and spiritual understanding coexist with recognition and compassion.

The minute you begin to access multidimensional reality, the whole thing begins to spin within its hologram. As the spiritual energy spins into the emotional body, it creates a centrifugal force that will spin off that which does not have life, so that the truth can emerge, so that the experience, the creative force, can be palpated by that being.

What happens is that the energy has to move through the entire chakric system and feed the pineal gland, which feeds the genitals in the physical. That which is unmanifest begins to feed the physical. People begin to relate with each other on those levels and as they relate, the capacity to expand experience increases.

A person who is without sexual feelings, like a woman who cannot feel her sexuality or a man who is impotent, will begin to center, to come to joining, because the separation will be released. We can experience the energy in the physical form which says, "Oh, yes. Here I am. I am here and here and here," and feels it on those high, tingling octaves of ecstasy. Those confusions and blockages we have on all levels of our sexual understanding can be released.

It takes a tremendous amount of energy to isolate ourselves in one area—to freeze the sexual energy. To become impotent or frigid or whatever those terms are that say, "I don't live here; I don't relate to this" is the energy which produces the wear and tear that causes death.

Once we begin to activate our conscious awareness in experiencing sexual essence, that separation will dissolve, and we will embrace the energetics of those feelings, so that a woman or a man will experience the nature of sexual energy. The energy is there within the structure that carries it forth and yet beyond the structure that carries it forth.

Yogis have embraced the word "celibacy," meaning that the sexual energy should not run outside the body, but that the sexual energies should run up through the body. If we understand that, we can see "conception" as a recognition of consciousness to radiate out from our bodies so that there is no separation. There is a great, great difference. In other words, if the vehicle that you're utilizing is an extension of your own physical form, and if your consciousness can come to that place, then there is no distraction from enlightenment; there is no separation of God-self. Celibacy is based on the rule that we must not despoil the body, which comes from the limitation of our recognition or capacity to access energetic form. We had to have the law that said, "Don't use your sexual energy, because you won't be able to get to the divine with it if you spend it out of the body." It is dependent upon a structure in which we needed those kinds of rules, because our consciousness could not extend to the vehicle in its entirety, i.e., all its subtle, interconnecting bodies of consciousness. Our consciousness, our sexual reality, was not a reality of enlightenment. It was locked in the lower chakras.

We have needed the doctrine of celibacy so that we would not confuse ourself with another self, so that we would not project so far out of our own body that we couldn't find this inner experience, our vertical access. Yet that's where we are now. We have projected so far outside of ourselves that we have profound confusion. We feel that we cannot experience the divine gift of life, of creative force, without somebody else being there.

Let us now awaken by utilizing the sexual energy, to expand the consciousness so that it can palpate sexual reality on a higher octave and bring people closer. It is not for us, at this time, to shut down that energy and live only in isolated form. The divine is moving through form, and we are simply to bring it full circle so that our chakric systems allow that energy to flow throughout.

Let's put that in yogic terms. If one is saying that we must not have masturbation or spilling of energy, it is not the spilling of energy itself that is the problem. The problem is in the *capacity* to utilize the energy, because universal law says that matter, or energy, is never wasted. Energy issues forth, whether it is on a thought-form mind level, or a sperm level or heart level or whatever level. We must allow the energy to flow forth and be channeled around so that it nourishes us. We must allow the pulsation in and out, which continues to create the motion that allows for the vertical access.

In practical terms, if we are discussing all this with someone who is seeking understanding on a sexual level, we talk about the fluid as the conductor of the energy. Our tendency has always been to close down, to shut off, because we can't handle that higher frequency. We can not hold the orgasmic state. We have to learn to hold the orgasmic state so that we allow energy to pass through the chambers of transmutation, through the channels, and continue to stay in contact with it as it moves up the chakric chain.

First, you may have sperm flowing out, and then you have the essence of the energy that has been released. Consciousness reaches out and takes the energy that has been released and draws it into this multidimensional, multibodied vehicle, so that it is not sent out away from this system through which it has been channeled. The same with the female. When the fluid is there, and the fluid mixes, then the female can draw it in, experience the frequency of that energy, and continue to draw it through the system up to the crown chakra. As it goes up to the crown, it will go up through all the chakras and wash the entire body. Then our consciousness can release the separation that says, "I am female," or "I am male," or "I am human," or "I am body," and go into that point of conception, which is the center out of which all things radiate even before entering thought.

I am speaking to you of an octave that we have hardly embraced in our definition of enlightenment. The idea is to experience all octaves of consciousness and not to isolate out form—matter from thought, matter from divine, matter from energy. They are all intertwined. They are all woven together in that wonderful, intricate patterning which is the latticework, which is the whole.

When you move away from the concept of left and right, good and evil, black and white that says, "One should not do this and one should do that," you find the energy. The second you come into the experience of that merging energy, all of the separation disappears. It gets spun out by the centrifugal force.

There are laws on all octaves throughout all bodies. There are laws on how to merge that are part of physical law. For example, anal penetration would be contrary to body law, because the anus is designed to expel wastes from the body. It's that simple. Disregarding that fundamental expression of body purpose causes disease on the physical level. We have to understand the pulsation of energy, how it is supposed to be moved through the body.

Is there any body law that describes caressing another body that's the same as yours as unhealthy? I don't think so. It's just using an outside person to caress you in the same way you would caress yourself. But when we begin to palpate that there are guidelines, we can experience them within ourselves. When something feels that it has the right flow, then it has the right flow. When something feels awkward or uncomfortable or imbalanced, then it's not the right flow. And when we go ahead and participate in it, then we are not choosing self, and we are not being discerning. If we are not listening, the body as cosmic teacher will start talking louder. The dissonance is called disease.

The way we at The Light Institute deal with homosexuality, or other issues which seem confusing, is to go into the realms of what it produces. How does the person experience reality through homo-sexuality? It is only a vehicle of self-expression. It has to do with who we attract to us, what feels right, where we're able to merge, and whether or not we go into fear states. When someone comes to me for whom homosexuality is an issue, our exploration has to do with that balancing within and how to take something that's internal, such as feminity, and express it in the physical vehicle. Shuffling through all the vehicles often produces the wobble. Something may be OK on an internal level, but it doesn't come out OK on an external level.

You will always be attracted to something that is going to create change within you. You may draw a person to you with whom you have tremendous karma, which is the thread of similarity between you. That person may be someone who has been destructive to you in another time. Your sexual connection is very strong, but it is still within that likeness, since we are a million threads; we are a lattice-work; we are a hologram. So where is it in that hologram that the stimulus is activated or created? In outside life, people often can only experience in the lower chakras, can only combine bodies, can only merge mentally or only in some other way. But in sessions, we can move around the hologram so that people can understand that it's the conception, it's the merging of the unmanifest with the manifest, that we seek. We have to learn how to contact each other through our chakric system, so that when we merge sexually, something takes place that gives the lift and doesn't just create that horizontal spin-ning-out.

As a species, we are entering a time-and-space octave where we can release patterns which are not growth-producing or purposeful for us now. But we must also honor what the physical body is telling us, so that we do not forget physical law as we explore the many levels. We can and must embrace a higher law, so that we can understand that we don't need to function just on these lower octaves.

The physical vehicle, if it is to survive, must move into the light body. It's going to have to quicken its frequency, or it will not be able to withstand the radiation which we are being exposed to now. Only as the vehicle quickens the frequency and is able to use the sexual energy which is the thread through all the subtle bodies, through all the realities, can we insure survival, because this frequency produces life.

When the spiritual energy moves in and the consciousness is able to embrace or experience it, then there is a liberation, and the energy rushes up through the chakric system. When that happens, the judgment cannot be held, because the experiential is released. We can only experience judgment when we are isolated in positionality. It is our positionality that creates judgment.

If we work within our own energetic system, then we will release separation. When we release the separation between the higher octave and the lower octave, we allow all of the chakric system to move. Then we will radiate that out to every person with whom we come into contact. We need to increase our sexual energy, not repress or block it, but we need to watch how we channel it. Our healing energy will increase, our creative energy will increase, our genius-capacity will increase. We will experience sexual and physiological magnification of energy, because we are triggering from the unmanifest. It is glandular triggering which will stimulate the entire urogenital tract, so that our sexual energy as we experience it in our bodies will increase.

At this time, don't rush out and find a partner to relieve the sexual energy because the octave is so high. That is what happened to sexual energy in the first place, when we could not handle the electromagnetic frequency of the orgasmic state. You can learn to draw it up through your own body to enhance the higher chakras, promote health, and experience ecstatic heights of your own creation. Think how this would revolutionize the dependent, powerless forms of interpersonal relationships!

All this has evolved from the '60s and '70s, when we began embracing sexual energy, exploring it, and breaking down some of our old thought-forms about it. We attempted to use that energy on each other, and we had this liberation of "I'll make love to everybody." That created a lot of disease, because it wasn't within the universal law as we applied it. We're reaching up now and asking, "What is the law?" We can begin to say that sexual energy comes up, and we can use it. Children have profound sexual energy; however, with children it's not located in any one place, so it radiates out through their hands and throughout their bodies. Their auric fields are filled with energy, and that's their sexual energy. It is the same as the healing or creative energies. That's the reason children are antsy. It's their sexual energy, and they have tremendous energy to run and play and spin and dance. But we don't, because ours is being sucked out through the lower chakras.

We need to be able to diffuse our sexual energy in that same way, so that it flows from us to some degree. Again, pure life force creates a movement. We now need to know that's all right, rather than controlling the energy. As adults, we move into the energy, and it drops right down into the lower chakras, and that's the way we experience sexual energy as denial.

In the future, we will have a merging of the male and female on this planet that we've never known, such things as commitment and responsibility and marriage will lose all their connotations, will all cease to exist because it will not be necessary. It will not be a force of resistance — "God, can I stand you for 10 years or 30 years?" or "Must I make a commitment?" — but the recognition of souls that learn how to dance through each other. We are each great mirrors of each other, great teachers to each other, and we can use that. It is our wont to dance. We love to mirror off each other. Let that mirroring become of the highest octave, so that as you look out of yourself, you see both the male and the female in that other being. You see the wholeness of that other being, so that you can merge without resistance, without fear of being consumed by the yang force or overwhelmed by someone else.

It's a very exciting time to look at sexual energy outside of all the unspeakables and face it, face what it is. It is the most exquisite, powerful energy that the material world has to access, because it's the closest energy to the unmanifest, to spirit. Once we learn how to see it that way, then we will know how to palpate it at that octave, instead of being locked into a very physical, slow-vibrating energy that has nothing to do with the heart. When we can bring the energy from the lower chakras up into the heart, up into the higher octaves, we can have the most profound experiences on this planet.

This is why we have great things to learn from disciplines like yoga, which begin to clear the chakric system so that that which is the slowest vibrating energy can become the fastest vibrating. We treat our physical bodies as if they are the slowest, densest, and most despicable part of ourselves. They are not. These vehicles are our greatest gift, and they need to be used in a sacred way. That sacred way begins with how you merge or even touch another person. On some planets, beings never touch. We have a wonderful physicality here, and we have to learn how to use it with the energy of our heart, with the energy of love. When we do, we will not have disease any more.

Every great, seeing body that has ever been on this planet, whether in a religious order or whatever, has always understood the power of sexuality, which is why he or she was adamant at making sure nobody used it. Because if anybody does, that person has the opportunity of breaking through the barrier. It is very hard to be focused on your finite, controlling mind at the moment of orgasm. It is the threshold of another dimension.

There's nobody out there influencing the body but you. Until you can own your body, forget what someone else is going to do for you. This is what happened in the '60s. We thought, "Well, my problem is this wife that I've been with for 20 years. I'm bored." We thought we could find the stimulus in a new being. It's not there. We found that out. How could we not have found that out? You can make love to a different person every day, and you will still feel unfulfilled, and you will not be orgasmic. The stimulus is not out there in the other person, and it doesn't matter how beautiful the body or how well you do the technique. That's irrelevant. The energy, as it moves, is moving in you. So be conscious when you make love, when you use your sexual energy.

Our sexual energy is within every cell of our body; it's not locked down in the genitals. This is one of the most fascinating things that has happened since we began to play with this sexual dance of who is it—me and you and all of you. It has produced the kind of disease that we have today because we thought it was locked down in the genitals. But, in fact, the conception takes place, and every cell that is created after that has that sexual imprint. When we draw that energy up, we can use it to be great healers. It's not any different from healing. It's the life force. It's called divine; it's called God. It's simply a force of energy with which we now can awaken our consciousness to understand and to utilize. It's in our fingers, in our hands. So we have to learn to palpate it within ourselves. You're not going to get there with anybody else until you get there with yourself.

If you're not orgasmic, if you're a person who makes love and you're not orgasmic, it is because you are denying your life force. You have not merged with your body. You are still running old thought-forms—"This is disgusting. This is not God. This is not good." God is ecstatic; God is orgasmic; God is life force. There's nothing stopping us from that except the belief that it is all in the genitals. Whenever we feel that orgasmic energy, that electromagnetic energy, that electric frequency that comes up in the orgasm state, we need to draw it up in ourselves, take it for ourselves, and allow the top of our crown chakra to radiate with that energy. That's what the sexual energy is. It's a vehicle that helps us tune the body to those frequencies. That's what it's there for. It's not to create separation or to be good or evil or any of those things, but it is accessible to us, and it is one of the few things that we can all experience.

One of the wonderful things that has happened with past-life work is that whenever someone sees someone they love, the reaction is, "Ahh. I have known them before. I have this magnetic attraction." I have to answer this magnetic attraction. We think it's down in the genitals, and lo and behold, it's up here in the heart. The knowing is in the heart. We've all known each other before. When you have that electromagnetic response with somebody, check it out on the level of merging. So often, when two people come together physically, they turn around and walk away without even recognizing that they know each other. They create new separation instead of love, instead of merging, because they're always projecting outside themselves. You cannot merge until the heart opens. And the collective heart has not opened. The heart has not yet opened on this planet. Now we can use this sexual energy to be the most exquisite tuning fork that we have on the physical level.

Perhaps some of you have had the experience of "cosmic orgasm," of having that energy come up within you. Once you have that experience, then the whole male-female thing falls apart. It's incredibly freeing. You don't need a partner, and you can't really get it from your partner. But you can help each other. If you become conscious with your sexuality, you can focus, for example, on the fluids that are there. It's a part of us. There are fluids in our bodies. As you exchange those fluids, notice that they are holding electricity; they're holding the electromagnetic energy of merging, of coming into body. They are holding the electric frequency of the unmanifest.

Instead of focusing on the end result, as something you're trying to get out there or as a release of energy or tension, lift up your consciousness and focus on a more refined level. The key to doing this is to move to those frequencies, into the electricity. The new age has been called the age of electric fluidity; that's exactly what it's about. Move into those frequencies, and you will experience an understanding of conception. With that, a tremendous freeing from all of the do's and don'ts will occur as you play it out in the outside world. It's of yourself. It's from yourself, and it's a great energy. You can use it in so many ways—in your hands to heal, in your throat to speak love, etc. Unless we use it, we're going to have disease. All disease is contraction, constriction, congestion of energy. You can focus your energy totally if you understand the mechanism of the body.

Sexual energy is the primary energy that propels us into this dimension. As we begin to understand the meaning of that, we will then take up that tool of manifestation and propel into this dimension those healing powers that will raise the dead, that will get rid of radiation, pollution, distress, and disharmony. Sexual energy is a great energy. Expand your thought-forms, expand your consciousness as to what it means, what it is.

Our work at The Light Institute is to embrace the sexual issue and remind people that we are multidimensional. Our whole internal relationship in defining self has a million options. For instance, we don't have to define or discuss homosexuality in terms of "Is that OK?" or "Is it not OK?" Instead, we see how someone is using it in relationship to the themes, or choices, they have made in this lifetime. It's not whether you are dancing sexually with a partner of the same body, because as multidimensional beings we've had many bodies, and we have many ways of merging with others. First of all, recognize that the choice of homosexuality, the choice itself of merging only with like kinds, is not as interesting as how it is teaching the person to grow. The truth is that even the concept of merging is outside the range of present human experience, regardless of sexual preference. If we could delve into "the anatomy of merging" with even one of our several bodies and experience its essence, all confusion and disease would disappear!

If a person is using homosexuality and experiences separation, confusion, and guilt, then that pattern of separation, judgment, and guilt, is being run in his or her own multidimensional reality. Sexuality is only one way to play it out. It's a very primordial way to work it out, yet it is very linked with spirit.

Our sexual energy is closest to our spiritual energy, so we have to look at how we present our sexual energy in relationship to how connected or disconnected we are to our spiritual energy. Otherwise, it's just a way to express our separation. The fundamental separation in our lives is that between ourselves and our God-selves. A sexual encounter without merging echoes the most profound emptiness imaginable. It is interesting that prepubescent children rarely experience loneliness. It is only after puberty awakens the kundalini, which is so misunderstood, mischanneled, and misguided into sexual activity, where our precious essences are spilled and hollowed, that we feel the abject aloneness characteristic of teenage years. It has to do with that conversation of self about male and female. Whether that's a confusion or an understanding depends on what it creates in our lives. If it creates love and merging, then it's an understanding. Homosexuality deals directly with male and female energetics seeking expression in the body. On some octave, on some level, homosexuality has to do with a spiritual understanding that can be very advanced. What does it or any other sexual positionality produce in a person's reality? We are not our sexuality, just as we are not our hatreds, our intellects, or our bodies. They are all tools we select to hone our experience of the "all."

In Chinese medicine, everything is related to everything else. The yin cannot survive without the yang, so the polarities must merge or there is no coherent life. The issue in any kind of sexual discussion has to be, "What are you creating for yourself with this?" One of the main difficulties with homosexuality has been that it so often over-activates the yang, controlling energy. It's an imbalance of carrying out an image of the yang force, when really it's the yin that's crying inside. When we have a person like that to work with, we want to palpate, "Where's the hunger? What is it that is not being nourished?" and start working back.

By coming into the body, we polarize into male or female, and then by virtue of that polarity, we attempt to express the sexual issues via that polarity. We attempt to satisfy our need via that slowest vibration of the first chakra, but it will never work. So we must infuse the spiritual energy to allow it to kindle the sexual energy with a different potency. Not only would it blast the first chakra open and therefore liberate the anger, separation, and feeling of "I must protect

112

myself," but then it would cause the energy to rise, nourishing all the other chakras and allowing that new potential to come into merging in terms of sexual contact, which is the highest octave of the physical.

Because there is no impregnation of spirit, because the unmanifest, the soul, is not finding enough expression, because the soul is only expressing under the dictate of the emotional body rather than its God-source, rather than its creation—the physical body does not demonstrate the light. We are ready to learn to do that now. We sense that is why we were created. If we don't, we will simply die.

We are light bodies, and we are in a transitional stage now where we can move through liquidity. It is liquidity that is allowing us to move into the physical, so that the body can purify the liquids and allow the light to enter. It is the divine purpose, the divine pattern, for the physical body to do that. It is simply the emotional body's weight, the impregnation of the emotional body that blocks that, and because it is a closed circuit, the emotional body then orchestrates and controls the mind. The ego hooks into the mental body, and the mental body can go on and on down this path or that path. "It's because of this; it's because of that." This is all a horizontal action. The mental body is in fact helpless, because the emotional body is not giving it the cues. It is not giving it the frame of reference that allows it to explore the vertical access.

Our vertical access is our sexual energy moving through our bodies, moving up through the chakras to connect us to the source. If we choose it, we are ready to feel that ecstasy. We are ready to blast through our sexual confusions, our emotional addictions. We are ready to merge with the divine, with the unmanifest, with our own higher self.

◇

EIGHT
THE CHILD
WITHIN

*People's own
wisdom will heal them;
people's own innate
knowledge will bring them
into balance.*

Now it is time to discuss the images, the spin points, that move us into other dimensions, other octaves. We use them to palpate, to register with our consciousness that which is untouchable, unseeable, unperceptible from our normal human perspective. The two spin points we work with are *the child within* and *contacting the higher self.*

As each soul spins around its intentionality, it creates matter and comes into form. The child that is born is an open bridge to the unconscious, to the unmanifest, expanded multidimensional soul. Babies are so magnificent. They're always staring off into space, into the eyes of their beloveds, of their companion souls, of God. We have all heard it said that the eyes are the windows of the soul, and the soul is very present in children. When you look into children's faces, you see the past lives they've had; you can see the karma. You can see a child that is happy and a child that is not—you can see the knowing within the child as it moves.

As we touch the child inside ourselves, we begin to access that bridge. Maybe it shut down in you when you were two; maybe it shut down in you when you were seven. It's not dead, it's just disconnected from you. It's just encased like a butterfly within a cocoon, and as all the great teachers have said, "Become the child, and you will know God." When we access the child, we go deep into the emotional repertoire. We ask the person to bring forth an image of the child within so that we can access that bridge of expansion which carries us into simple joys. We find realities that we can record and understand, and most importantly, that we can access experientially, because what's the purpose of another dimension if it's not accessible to us? What's the purpose of something we perceive if it's not happening in us now, if we're not able to use it in this dimension? The child is very inventive; it never wastes experience.

Now for the first time in our history, we have the ability to access those levels, those dimensions in which we can precipitate the unmanifest into these vehicles, into this reality, and create on a level we have never ever done before. Accessing those octaves is very important, and bridging them is even more important. It's not going to do any good to be spaced out someplace, to reach for that drug you hope will do it for you, because you will just tear holes in the auric field. There is no hope for assimilation of the uncharted wealth available to us in the unmanifest, unless we can access it through our clear intention and bring it into this world.

There is no external access to your inner self. There is only your inner self nudging and pushing and hollering and waiting—always waiting for you to spin around the hologram of your being and focus your attention in order to precipitate those knowings, those dimensions which remind you of Godliness.

As we begin to visualize and extend our tools of perception, we find that symbols are the language of the unconscious. As we draw forms from this great swirling pool, we give form to the formless so that we can move into those octaves of translation, into increments of meaning that we can utilize as the fuel for our expansion, for our growth. We can come into the experience of the child, because the child is the closest, most intimate, palpable, living symbol. It is the same time-bridge that allows the emotional body to make contact with the higher self, to make contact with the soul. As the great masters have said, "Follow the little children." By fusing with the child within us, we are able to expand the emotional body's repertoire, allowing the child to go from experiences of fear, anxiety, and imbalance, and move into a balanced state. We begin to learn the technique; we begin to learn the pathway, learn that we can, at any moment, rebalance our own selves. Thus we have that connection to our divine higher selves.

When we speak of the child, we speak of that living bridge which is the wisest being we can make contact with on this plane. The child is simply once removed from our physicality, because we have all been children, and we all have those memories of our childhood—those experiences of the emotional body which are palpable and still radiating from us. Those experiences have consolidated and crystallized the imprints upon which we are operating as our frame of reference for who we are, and what we are allowed in our life today. When we make contact with that entity, we are able to shift the blueprint from the emotional body's experience to the deeper, more profound love of our cosmic self. The child reminds us that God laughs.

The emotional body first makes contact with the child. In working with the child—which is palpable, which is close to us and recognizable, which is not outside our present frame of reference even to the mental body, to the finite mind—we then are able to prepare ourselves to move into the next vehicle, the octave of expansion which is contacting our higher selves. The child is a very central personage to us and always triggers a level of emotional release, because all of the images and experiences that we remember from our childhood are encased in that entity that we call "the child within." Through its purity we re-establish our link with natural, ecstatic states: wonderment, rapture.

On rare occasions, a person will bring up a child within who is of the opposite sex. When that happens, several things may be going on. One is that a prior lifetime is impinging, and the consciousness of the person is still attached to that other lifetime. Very often there was a lifetime where the person went out early, perhaps dying as a baby or a child, and the person is still confused in this lifetime. Many times the spirit, which is the astral composition, is locked in the astral dimension, so the consciousness just comes in with the same body it had when the person left before. But that's not where the soul is. People may view themselves as bodies they had before if they left those bodies early, but the soul resides in this life. Sometimes the child within of another sex is speaking to their bisexuality from a previous life as the opposite sex.

If the child within comes out as the opposite sex, we delve into it, watch where it comes up, and explore it during past-life sessions. We can begin to heal that split right there, which is incredible. If the person is female and she brings a boy up, is she seeing it as a boy-child because she has an imprint that says, "You were supposed to be a boy"?

Perhaps all the way through the pregnancy the mother was saying, "This has to be a boy." As that woman gets on the healing table and begins to speak to her unconscious, it says, "Well, I'm a boy. I have to be. Otherwise I'm not going to be loved, I'm not going to be received." We want to palpate the source of that. Is it coming from sexual confusion? Is it coming from parental imprint? Is it coming from a yang force that simply sees the child as a boy? We let her experience herself as a boy and give the child a gift. And when the child receives the gift, we watch to see if the child turns into a girl. Once a child goes into a balancing state or is allowed to express its own sexual nature, a switch can take place.

We have to view what it means to be homosexual or to view our sexual activity from the spiritual octave, from an expanded perception. When we look at the hologram, the akashic record of someone, then that judgment or fear changes. We view each person that we're working with holographically. We are dealing with an emotional body. We are dealing with a spiritual body. We are dealing with physical, mental bodies. All of those bodies are interwoven, yet they are separate. They each have their own consciousness. We cannot pass a judgment or view reality as only one body, because it is moving with all those others. They are all in concert with each other, though we may be totally unconscious of them.

That's what we're here to do, to interweave the bodies so that we have an integral vehicle through which a person can manifest unmanifest spiritual energy, or manifest pure thought, physical activity, or emotional vibration. This is crucial. We must be cognizant of every person we address, listen to, and touch on four levels, at least four dimensions. Those four are the ones we are playing with from our conscious capacities.

We call that *enlightenment*, but our idea of enlightenment is kindergarten. We have to be able to work with those four frequencies. Every time we touch a physical body, we are touching a past life, we are touching a multidimensional being, we are touching the spirit. And we have to tune our hands to that understanding so that when we touch someone, we feel. What is the emotional body saying through this vehicle, through designing a vehicle that's fat or thin or tall or short or whatever it is? It's expressing itself, it's expressing its emotion, its spirit. We have to be aware of its meaning so that we can guide that

118

person around the circle. We always must be aware of polarity; it's such a contraction. It does not encompass truth.

It is our job to help people experience truth by expanding them. People always see the impossible: "If only I were _____, then I could be _____." We have to break them of that pattern. We have to help them to decrystallize themselves from those encapsulations that lock them onto whatever octave it is. It doesn't matter if it's a mental octave or an emotional or physical octave. If a person has a child within of the opposite sex, we know we're dealing with this, and we have to help them heal it. Each of us must accept our choice of body. Ultimately, by the end of the session, they will see themselves in the same body. Because if they see themselves only in male bodies and they are females, there can be no resolution. There will be no merging. There will be separation, and there will be judgment, and they'll be stuck.

Eventually, people take in the child, no matter what the child is, although it will have gone through different transmutations. Normally, the child will make that transmutation as soon as it becomes identified in its wholeness. If a child within a male person is female, then the energetic balancing is very profound. Hopefully it will have led itself through a progression. In other words, the child would have initially asked for a gift that would have allowed for the female, yin energy to come forth. If the child were working with color, it would ask for a yin color, something that would symbolize that balancing.

People's own wisdom will heal them; people's own innate knowledge will make the choice that will bring them into balance. That's why I talk about "leading the witness." All we want to do is lead them into the place where they can do the work they need to do themselves; we need not interfere. We're just creating the hologram through which they can circle and begin to spiral until they get what they need. And they're always going to choose it. The choices people make are breathtaking, the symbols they ask for, the gifts that they ask for, and the colors need never be suggested from the outside.

People choose just what they need every time. Every past life that they ever go into will be just what they need. If they need to be flashy in this lifetime, they'll get ten lifetimes of being the peon until they understand they don't need the glamour.

When the child speaks to us from wisdom, when the child speaks to us of knowing and merges into our consciousness by re-entering our present experience, there is a profound healing that automatically takes place—a lifting of the hook from the emotional body. It is perhaps the first experience of merging with the self, because, when we are actually experiencing our childhood up until a certain stage, we have those doors open to our higher selves, to our divine selves. As children, we move in and out of our bodies. Our consciousness moves into other frequencies and other octaves until about the age of seven. Then the presence of our peers, the presence of our daily life, become formulated in our consciousness to a certain degree, and we then funnel into our third-dimensional presence, moving further and further away from our multi-dimensionality. Up until that time, we have more freedom. It's like watching the baby who stares into space, moving its consciousness easily in and out, to this world or to another world.

When we merge with that child as an entity of wisdom who understands why we're here, who understands what we need for balance, it is a very emotional experience, allowing us to draw our attention from our ego or outer consciousness, to an inner place of contacting those natural octaves of joy and wonderment. A child is naturally a being of wonderment, a being that experiences lightness, who does not hold pain. The child's frequency is too high to hold those darker, heavier emotions, even when the external world begins to impinge upon the child with adult imprints that the child records as anxiety, fear, anger. The natural state is to let go, to constantly let go, because the child lives in the brain patterning of the hologram. The child does not have that left-brain imprint in glue. Even if in one moment fear or anxiety is experienced, the next moment the child will move into a place of wonderment. The child within can give us that gift, return to us that memory, that experience of wonderment, which always lifts the octave of the emotional body. When we experience wonderment, we forget fear, and thus can embrace our divine selves. When we experience our divine selves, we let go of judgment. It takes place energetically. We can palpate it, experience it, recognize it. We begin weaving the hologram of our multidimensional selves.

By using the example of the child, we begin patternings which allow people to use a vehicle for that contact, get a handle on a way to move into those frequencies, those octaves. People can later return to those realities without the presence of a facilitator, without ritual, without any external impetus, but simply by returning to the child within. From that octave, we can then go on to introduce those higher levels of emotions which have not been present on this planet, those ecstatic states that are not as yet a part of our frame of reference. So the child within is a profound bridgeway in our evolutionary process.

◇

It was to be our first graduation ceremony at *The Light Institute*. We wanted it to be not only a celebration of a new beginning, but an exclamation point of our capacity to bring the ethereal realms into full view. We wanted to challenge ourselves on the level of manifestation. Since childhood I've always had a little streak in me that sought out the impossible, or miracles, because I have always known that some day we would perform miracles ourselves, just as it has been foretold.

With a twinkle in my eye, I proposed a firewalk. Firewalks are a perfect example of bringing into experiential reality the "impossibles" of our limited minds. I was delighted as my colleagues-to-be accepted the "initiation by fire."

Appropriately, I had already put myself through this kind of initiation and had walked a thrilling nineteen times before. To push the edge for myself, I vowed to be the first one across the fire. My firewalking instructor had told me that to be the first one across is very challenging, because the brain records everything it sees as possible, but without the initial frame of reference, that "seduction of the mind," a much higher level of focus is required. I not only wanted to place myself in that position of focus, but

I set for myself the intention of "gliding" effortlessly across the fire, rather than "crunching" across, as I had done before. I was not going to rush across—as if by moving faster, I could neutralize the effects of fear. I wanted to nullify my fear completely, to stroll across in a state of total grace.

We were all there doing the initial exercises to prepare ourselves. It was a group of about 45, which included three of my children: Karin, who was being initiated as a colleague; Megan, age thirteen; and Teo, age six. This was the hottest fire I had seen. The flames reached about fifteen feet up, and the person tending was standing far back from it. It took three hours for those flames to die down enough to create the bed of coals, which stretched out more than sixteen feet. I felt a moment of concern about whether my little Teo would be able to hold her concentration for such a distance.

We stood in a ring of clasped hands around the coals, which were by now glowing a beautiful yellow-white color. Though I knew by their color that they were at their hottest temperature, they seemed gentle and soothing to me, almost mesmerizing. I felt as if we were made of the same stuff. I broke the circle and stepped up onto the bed. Across my face I felt the dancing flicker of a burning log, which had not yet relinquished itself to coal. Fixing my sight on a spot at the other end, I began to pull myself towards it. I felt like a wind gently lifting and falling as I moved along the continuum, and, after a timeless moment, I stepped off onto the other side. Exhilaration and ecstatic joy swept through my being. I had to fight my body to keep from jumping into the air—but it was someone else's turn. To my surprise, Megan stepped to the edge. I remember how my breath and heart became stilled. I watched her young grace as she glided across with a sureness that brought tears to my eyes. She circled around to stand next to me and in a very strong, knowing voice said, "Mom, I'll never have to die of cancer. Maybe I'll never die at all!"

The depth and swiftness of her assimilation of the firewalking exercise took my breath away. People began to move more swiftly to the coals, and I felt an exhilarated energy-pattern begin to form itself. Teo suddenly grasped my hand and pulled me to the fire. We stepped up together and began our walk. About two-thirds of the way across, she whimpered, "Mom, it's getting hot." I answered, "You can do it, Teo, you can, you can," and we reached the end and jumped into the pool of water awaiting us. It was too much for me; I was so elated, I let out a little yell. Everyone was experiencing the same exuberance, and people began to join each other in twos and walk across the fire.

Even though a few people sustained some blisters, we all shared such a feeling of empowerment. We were truly a group of "untouchables." I remembered back to the early Peace Corps days, when we all experienced that untouchability. It was a feeling of belonging to something good and joyous: a force of light.

◇NINE◇

MANIFESTATION

The higher self is
the megaphone of the soul;
it can fill the emotions with
the flutter of the soul.

Bridging is crucial in this lifetime to bring forth the unmanifest into manifestation. We have the blueprints, our very bodies are the proof that we have the blueprints. We came from the nothing + thought, and then there was fluid, and then there was attraction between the male and the female. They merged and created the first cell. In that first cell is the encoding, and because of that original encoding, you and I are here today. It was all the genetic coding that you chose and all the memories from your past, present, future experiences, recorded in that ever-expanding consciousness that you chose as well. Conception is a meditation; it is the great wisdom.

We have come to a place on this Earth where we can focus on conception and manifest a flower. It's the same energy. It's pulling from the unmanifest, from the energy that's there, into form. This is our birthright. It has always been there, and that's how we got here. We have the recording on a cellular level. Meditate on a cell; meditate on the moment of conception, which is when the divine entered time and space, and the nothing became matter. That conception point is the middle point of the figure eight; it is the center of the universe. It is our spiritual energy. We need to remember that point. We need to focus on that so that we can bring the unmanifest into consciousness. We can use the child inside us to move back and forth across the bridge, because the child is not attached to its name. It's not attached to the outside world. It moves freely.

I remember many years ago I had a bilingual summer school in Galisteo, and we used a Silva mind-control technique as a project, because many of the children in town were failing school. We were interested in what children see when they look at other human beings.

We would look into the body of some stranger, and the kids would be twitching and wiggling and looking out the window and tapping their fingers. I'd say, "So what do you see?" And they'd say, "Oh, this man has a funny little black spot right in here." They didn't know the word for it, but they knew what was moving and not moving because they were always in that state of "seeingness." They could see illnesses in the body! They were always accessible to that bridging, able to reach up and see other realities. We adults still have that capacity buried within us. At any time, if we want to know something, we can reach up and see other realities too. We are complete.

There is nothing that I will say to you—or that anyone will ever say to you—that you don't already know. You just may have forgotten. It's just your higher self echoing for you, so that you can say, "I know that." And what is *knowing*? Knowing is living, experiencing, merging, being whole. When we merge the child within us, we access all there is, and we pull it into form. As we do this, we have choices. If we can stay away from our judgment, our egos, we can allow the knowing to come in as a pure energy, and we can shape it and create the reality.

We can use the concept—the actuality of conception—to stop an earthquake, to get rid of nuclear waste. How are we going to get rid of nuclear waste? Our technology is not complete enough. We've just come to the end of that level. We just did something we can't fix, like Chernobyl. What are we going to do now? Dematerialize it, because that's the only choice we have. The threshold between the manifest and unmanifest worlds allows matter to pass both ways. We are now in a place where if we do not use the higher mind that we have, we will not survive. We all know that.

It's an exciting time; it's a most magnificent time. It is the moment right now for which we were born, every one of us. If any of you think you're too old, forget it. You're not going to leave until you complete everything now. We have come to a point now where we must quickly finish up our attachment to personal karma and begin to focus in unison within that great pulsation that creates life. That is cosmic law. We can manifest, because that's the reason each and every one of us has chosen to be alive at this time, to break the karmic addition of birth, struggle, and death.

We already have the secret of altering death, of altering aging. We

128

understand enough about molecular structure now, but we haven't got it through the hologram, because we're so busy in our puny little finite minds going from left to right forever. We never figure out what life's about, what it is saying to us. We must close the circle. We must bring it around and understand that the information we have now is enough. It's enough. It's time. We need now to access that information from a living, experiential place, which means that there is nothing outside ourselves that we are not participating in, that we cannot design or redesign.

We do not have to be starving, or suffering droughts or pollution. But we're not going to fix it with machines, with the Atlantean mentality. We're going to use the pure, divine energy in us that is latent. We must begin to access that total consciousness, so that we can make those choices that are vital to us at this time.

In 1985, I took an 82-year-old Hopi woman to Africa, to Somalia, to call the rain, because Africa was experiencing a tremendous drought. The Hopis of Arizona have been calling the rain for 4000 years to grow their corn. They live in an arid land and grow corn, blue corn, using the same seed they had 4000 years ago. They still have the knowledge. They support themselves, are peaceful, and listen to the universe.

It was the first time that a woman had done this particular ritual. It was always kept for the men. Her brother was the last son of the last sun chief of the Hopi. He said, "I am a Hopi medicine man, I must hold the Earth here at Hopi, so I will send you." For the first time in 4,000 years, an 82-year-old woman took the increments of Hopi consciousness with her to Africa. She marched out there amongst all the Somalians into their cornfields, and she said, "I bring you this seed which I grew myself, so that you may know that you never need to go hungry. And I will now call the rain, so that you may know that you never need to be without water." She prayed, and down came the rain. It rained so much for three days that we couldn't get back to her shrine, where we were to have gone every day to bless it with sacred corn meal. The Hopis have an expression that says, "When the heart is pure, it will rain." She didn't want any fuss. She didn't want anyone to take pictures. She just wanted to make rain and go back home, and that's what she did.

The international meteorological monitors tracked the storm

which had come from a direction that never normally brings rain. It crossed Ethiopia and the Sudan exactly where she directed it, from Somalia. We pride ourselves in our technology, yet we are helpless, we are disconnected from the life-bearing forces of this planet. This woman, this *being*, demonstrated the solution. If you need rain, call the rain. Bring your heart into focus, in harmony with the seasons, with the Earth, with the beings, with the sky. The sky is a live organism in the same way the ocean is a live organism. Simply allow yourself, and you can bring rain.

At our school, we used to get the little children out to bang on tin cans, and they always brought the rain, too. There's nothing magical about manifestation; it has to do with the harmonics of intention. Most of us feel so guilty about our experiences with manifestation in other lifetimes that we don't allow ourselves to participate directly. Witness the Atlanteans. They learned to work with manifestation, and ended up using their crystals to blow up their civilization. We may do it again if we don't learn the lessons pertaining to personal power. We are in an evolutionary spin now, which will either bring us to extinction, because we have become emotionally disassociated from our environment, or will move us up into a higher frequency. If we attune our emotional bodies to a level wherein we can acknowledge participation in our personal lives to the whole world, we will begin to experience a new and powerful centering. We have got to get beyond using only ten percent of our brains, mostly the linear, left-brain side. We can't manifest with just part of the brain. We have to learn how to use the brain holographically, then the brain will radiate comprehensive harmony into our entire environment and into the universe.

When we can palpate our center, we can manifest anything with that energy. In our work at The Light Institute, we focus a lot on the child, our own child within, because it allows us to come to a place where we can palpate that bridge—the child and multidimensionality. We can move when we're not so crystallized into who-we-think-we-should-be that we can't get out there and explore the rest of our multidimensional selves.

From the vantage point of accelerated frequencies, we can reorganize the structure of the hologram. This eliminates our insistence on the linear viewpoint. Linearity is the insistence in the brain that it access only ten percent of its potential, ignoring the ninety percent that brings that linear energy around to the hologram, that allows us to see all. It is cosmic law that everything pulsates—in and out, in and out, life and death, death and life. Our spines pulsate, our bodies pulsate, our organs pulsate, our glands pulsate. All we have to do is take our consciousness, which is rushing around to see if we're OK or not, and focus our attention on that pulsation. Then we will begin to move across the bridge, and we will begin to recognize the divine at that level. Thus we will recognize ourselves as consciousness itself, as a power of the soul which doesn't succumb to good and evil, to shoulds and shouldn'ts.

The child is the first wave of the bridge to the multidimensional self. The next wave from the child is cognition of the higher self. The higher self is, in a way, that fountain from which all things flow. It is the place you can go in order to move into your center, in order to know, "This is it; I am it"—in order to validate your reality, to come into contact with yourself. The higher self is the self as it merges with the divine. It is a composite of the individual soul and the universal soul. The higher self can access at all times all knowing within the divine, creative force and feed it back to the individual self.

The higher self is not, in fact, an entity. I describe it as the megaphone of the soul. It is the mechanism for precipitating the unmanifest into manifestation so that we can create a thought-form, so that we can ascertain the answer, so that we can recognize the path. The higher self gives us form. It can speak to the mind and say, "Yes, it's this." Or it can speak to the emotion and fill the emotions with the flutter of God. Or it can speak to the body and allow the body to be limitless, allow the body to be light. It is that which stirs the pure God force within our human aspect of being. It is the point at which we ourselves and the God force merge. It is the center of the infinity symbol, the center of the figure eight. That point is the threshold to the higher self, from which we can access all knowing, that can allow us to experience ourselves—whether physically or emotionally or mentally—as part of universal love, so the higher force can move through our various aspects, and we can experience ourselves creating our lives.

The higher self is not an aspect of seduction; it is not a particle of the astral dimension. What is wonderful is that it is always there. When we first learn to contact the higher self, the level of our doubts reflect the degree of our separation, our experience of separation, our experience of guilt and judgment. Utilizing this megaphone of the soul is an art. It is something that we get better at as we develop trust, as we develop surrender, as we develop a frame of reference for merging back into universal flow.

Contacting the higher self is the most profound and important thing that we do at the Institute. Once people have access on any octave of their being, no matter how slight, no matter how much is blocked, they have a cognition and experience of that connection to their higher selves. They then have the tool that allows them to make that pivotal switch from victim to creator. And as we at the Institute help people contact their higher selves, we give them, literally, a survival mechanism, because they may not be able to discern or recognize truth or trust anything that is outside of their own inner being. They must have that bridge to the divine self, so that they can leap from the precipice and fulfill their destinies—not from a place of karma, but from a God-place free from the karmic cycle.

I speak of the higher self as a megaphone, as a bridge, so that we begin right from the beginning to understand that although we are isolated in one sliver of the hologram called the human self, the ego, that this is only one perspective, one positionality of our divine selves. This is very important, because when people first begin to contact their higher selves—since they are so enrooted in their self-recognition as a human—they often can only allow themselves to receive or to recognize the higher self in the way which all the great religions make so much fuss about, God being a human male. God is not limited to the role of a human male. But we see God as a human male through the sliver of our yang—our human, earthly perception of this moment.

The whole essence of our work is that we're attempting to find ourselves—find home, find God in ourselves. But as long as we see God as a human male, we limit it. We are trying to find the spiritual essence within ourselves which releases us from judgment and worldly preoccupation. Clients of the Institute may be totally embroiled in worldly concerns, and that's why we start, before they even get on the table, describing to them that *the emotional body is what's making the choices in this lifetime.* We've already begun to describe them as multidimensional beings, because we talk about the emotional body, the spiritual body, the physical body, and the mental body. That's the concept we give in the very beginning of the sessions—to help them understand that we all think we are living in our mental bodies, but we actually have these subtle bodies—the astral, the spiritual, etc. What we need to do is merge them so that we can make choices in our lifetimes that lead us into ecstasy, that lead us on to the higher octaves. It is the emotional body that is slowing us down while our minds, our intellects, have expanded tremendously.

Our physical bodies live longer now, and we are beginning to look for our spiritual energy. We recognize that there is a spiritual force, and we're looking for it, but the emotional body is lagging behind. The emotional body, because it is not in time and space, is really making our choices. It is the emotional body, radiating out so much of the content of our auric fields, which gives our message to the outside world.

The emotional body is what draws the world to us. For example, if a person wants a better job but doesn't feel worthy of a better job, then he or she will send out a message of unworthiness of a better job. What are the issues being brought up? Are they relationship issues, job issues, ego issues, spiritual issues? What are those issues the person has defined for us in the beginning. Then we can say, "The emotional body is radiating out the imprint of what you are going to receive. You think you need a different environment, a different job, but you radiate a message that says, 'Don't choose me, I can't really do this.'" That's how we continue the treadmill of karma, instead of progressing at the rate of which we are capable.

That's why we do past-life work. Actually, it has nothing to do with what's past. The emotional body is what keeps us on this treadmill lifetime after lifetime, continuing the patternings to which it is addicted. Often past-life sessions will allow people to look at something they will not look at in their lives now. Past-life work will access whatever those patterns were from the time they were two years old or imprints from other lives that the emotional body is holding now. Those patterns are choosing the quality of the life they are experiencing now.

At the Institute, we begin to quicken the emotional body, to move it, so that people can radiate from themselves messages that allow them to draw in new people and new situations, that lift them up, that bring them onto a new octave. That's the purpose of the work, to bring people into a recognition of their multidimensionality. Past-life work simply allows us to develop a bigger repertoire. What we find is that people don't receive or perceive a repertoire that isn't relevant to where they are now, and they are usually experiencing that repertoire with the same people they've known before. That's what helps us to clear relationships. If they can see it this way—"I'm in this kind of a relationship with this person. I've drawn this person in because of how I related to the individual before, or how I related to him or her in other aspects of my multidimensional being"—then they can see it in a new way. Once they see that, they are irrevocably changed. Our emotional bodies don't want us to change; they're not interested in our being happy or ecstatic; they're only interested in recording and repeating the repertoires that they already have.

Once the emotional body begins to expand or quicken, people are going to go through a profound change. Their relationships will change. Their lives will change, and they need to know that. In doing this work, they are already following the dictates of their higher selves. Their higher selves are already guiding them into this place to lift them into a new experience of themselves, and to divest them of experiences that aren't serving them now.

We all say, "I want to pick someone who will love me. I want to have a good relationship. I want to do these things." And yet, if we have someone who loves us and someone who doesn't love us, we're constantly seduced by the one who doesn't love us. We're bored by the one who loves us. We don't even see the one who loves us. We don't even acknowledge the love. Why? Because the emotional body likes the challenge and the seduction and the game of the one who isn't going to choose us. It's destructive because it pulls us into polarity; it pulls us away from our own selves.

The higher self comes in, and we can experience ourselves as a whole. We can get in touch with who we are, why we have chosen this lifetime, rather than the treadmill of "I can only find myself if I'm touching you, or if you're constantly reaffirming for me who I am." This causes jealousy, denial, and anxiety, which activates anger, etc. We bring up all the old repertoire of the emotional body. Every person who is here in this lifetime right now, in this pivotal piece of history on this Earth, has come to break that—to become who they really are. They already have some kind of a feeling that they have something to give, that there's something about who they really are that's not just "Who's doing the dishes?" "Who's making the money?" or "Who is living alone or being loved or not loved?" They're already palpating deeper sources, and that's why they come. We keep mirroring their quest for these sources and affirming that they know their quest. Because they do know their quest, they've already attained it within their blueprint, and now all they have to do is surrender into it.

It's not down the road; enlightenment is not down there someplace or in the eyes of a lover. Enlightenment is right here, where you can experience it now. This is very important, because when people get off the table, whatever they experience is it, it is the way to understand that they are palpating and quickening and changing their emotional bodies. By seeing or feeling those things, they have already begun a process of spinning upwards, an upward spiral that is going to change them, no matter what they think has happened.

When they go home, they're going to feel different. When they walk out the door, they're going to feel irrevocably different, and they are. We tell them they are going to go through a change, and they can view that with a cosmic giggle and can embrace the fact. Even if they're running around angry, they're suddenly going to start listening to their anger, start listening to their projection. We are giving them a vocabulary and an environment that allows the change to happen, and they just do it.

The higher self is the greatest concept in the world, because suddenly people have a handle on some vague sense inside themselves that has meaning, that has shape—a sense of the higher self. What does it look like? Maybe it looks like a triangle, and maybe it looks like a cloud, and maybe it looks like a figure in a cloak. But at least they get a handle on it, and it means something to them. That's tremendously profound.

We start teaching them our language, because our language is on a whole new octave of consciousness. We don't worry about trying to translate what is going on at the Institute into someone else's language system, because there is no frame of reference for it. Whether clients have been teachers, or meditated for ten years or been healers for ten years, most of them have had so many separations that they feel they need a translation. They begin to experience contraction in their emotional body or freeing up of their solar plexus, or for the first time they experience *crias*, energy moving through the body. These things give them a new consciousness that is precipitating their multidimensionality into their conscious life. People may think they are coming to us because they need to get rid of a relationship or they need to change something in their lives, but that's not why they're here.

We help them to experience themselves as multidimensional beings, and they are able to contact the divine in themselves. We give them a new frame of reference, and they can articulate it. They can feel it, they can experience it, they know how to get back to it. It's not like, "You have your higher self once, and you never get your higher self again." It's not like being in meditation and wondering if you're there. It is an operational, practical way of connecting people to themselves.

When people describe the unmanifest, they describe going home. They come into places where they experience the God within, where they do not experience separation. They often go into ecstatic states, because if you get out of the way, you'll go right into ecstatic states. It's you—your ego, your positionality, your emotional body—that's in the way. In that ecstatic state of wholeness, everything is there, nothing is missing. People recognize their god. I'll ask them, "Why did you separate?" They all say the same thing: "To gain experience." For some reason, there is a desire to manifest that knowing on a conscious level. That's the answer that's always given. "I wanted to separate out to experience something, to participate in that manifestation from some level of 'I.'" Then, as soon as they move into matter, all of these new laws take place. The laws of matter come into effect. We become seduced, basically, by that. We become more and more drawn into emotional bodies. We don't have emotional bodies in all of our multidimensional frequencies, and so it's very fascinating. We become more and more hooked in, saying, "Well, let me just see what those guys are doing over there." However, it wasn't a wrong decision to come here in these bodies. Now, as never before, we have the opportunity to bring the divine with us here and to manifest it. That's why we have chosen to come right now, every one of us—to manifest.

What is our role with the animal kingdom and the mineral kingdom? Again, we are not really separate. We're a part of the animal kingdom, we're a part of the mineral kingdom. We have this funny little thing where we say, "This is organic and this is inorganic," which of course is absurd. We are a part of every kingdom. We are not separate, and we need to merge. For example, the dolphins and the whales are beyond us. Their holographic brains perceive much more than ours.

Each time we work at the Institute, we go in deeper and begin to function on a soul level that knows who we are. We don't have to wait for some booming voice from a male god to say, "You are such and such." The holographic self is the most exquisite apparatus, the most exquisite symbol of our cognition. The people that I've worked with have given me such a great gift as they focus and as they attune to what we call our higher self. We like to think the higher self has to be a big deal, but the higher self is not. In fact, the images that come representing the higher self are simply the instrument of our consciousness attuning us into some connection, into some reality.

When people tune in to their higher selves, the image that they come up with tells me great stories about them. It tells me where their consciousness is at the time. It tells me what they need to push on, what they need to explore, what's going to happen, because their higher self is already cueing them. We are all receiving, in that other 90 percent of our brains, the cues of reality and the cues of truth all the time. It's just that we don't know how to pay attention, and that is why in all the ancient societies they did so much ritual—to focus in on getting those cues. They had an advantage over us, because they could listen to what it meant when the lightning struck. It had meaning. There is nothing in the universe that does not have meaning, is not synchronistic. The universe is not chaotic; it is a cohesive gentle course. If we stop to take a picture of our lives today, the picture may look very chaotic, like we're going in the wrong direction, but *there are no wrong directions.* We are simply linking up some wheel of the hologram, some spoke of the hologram, in order to function in that pulsating way.

The higher self is an emissary to the periphery. It is a translation for you of the unmanifest out there that has no symbols, that has no perspective, no positionality. It is simply a glimpse into that which translates close enough to you so that you can find the increment of meaning within it and open the mind. Our emotional bodies want us to see our higher self as a person, but the higher self comes in as a spinning wheel or a wind or as a triangle. It will come in as some symbol, poking at some level of your consciousness, saying, "Open this door." Inside yourself, on the other side of that door, you have an increment of meaning which you will then recognize on a soul level, and you will expand. I tell you this so that if you meditate, and you are lookᵧ ᵤor your higher self and you get a spinning wheel or a triangle and think you didn't get your higher self, don't worry. If you will, instead of trying to control it, allow yourself to just surrender into the essence of that symbol, you will be nourished in the most magnificent way. Your consciousness will change. Your brain will begin to record. It will begin to precipitate in patternings and realities that you don't normally focus on, and you will find meaning in this relating that allows you to expand and let go and grow.

The higher self, then, is that megaphone. It is that translation tool that helps us to get to a place where there are no images. It is nothing we can cognate with our linear mind; it is the multidimensional hologram. When you get a symbol of higher self, if you find yourself talking to a triangle, don't despair; triangles talk very clearly. For example, someone might say, "I asked my higher self a question, and all I got was this pink light." The image is telling you that the pink light is the trigger, is the veil through which you must pass in order to be able to perceive anything on the other side. Pink is the color of love; it's the color of rejuvenation. The higher self is telling you, "Clothe yourself in love; awaken, stimulate your life force, then you will have the courage to be who you are." The answer is there. The answer is simply given to you from the perspective of the other side of the hologram.

On the earth plane we become very habitual with definition, with our perception. Our perceptions have become very, very narrow. We have become caught up in linear thoughts. It is very important for us to begin to accept and perceive ourselves in an expanded way. We have been seduced by ritual. We have been seduced through earlier cultures by alchemy. There's a difference between alchemy and true manifestation. Alchemy is the forcing of the will on matter, and we can do it. The scientists are doing it now; we did it 5000 years ago; we did it 50,000 years ago, and in our inner memories, we all remember using that power. There's a price to pay for that kind of alchemy, for that kind of forcing someone to be who you want them to be, for that kind of "Let's make it be this way" or "Let's make it be that way." We're paying the price right now on this planet, and it is a very difficult exercise for us to let go of the seduction of alchemy, to let go of the will, of personal power.

Those are the entrapments that we came into at the time of the Atlanteans, where we found that if we focused that will, we could make it happen. In making it happen, we had a jolt which gave us a sense of personal recognition. We became so seduced by that jolt that we have yet to let it go, we have yet to surrender. That's one of the biggest challenges on this planet at this time, to let go of your personal power so that you can attain your true power, so that you can merge into the universal flow. It is a part of being able to understand, "Is it right to call the rain today, or am I a manipulator?" We have to begin to see the hologram. Otherwise, we're fiddling and will pay the price for fiddling, which we have done before and which we all remember.

It is a very important time to begin to understand that separation, to let go of that personal power, to let go of control. We are to recognize that we can attune to a higher frequency, to a higher octave, from which we can manifest what is good for the whole, not just what's good for the individual. Then we move back into the light, move back into that universal level from which all this world was created, all this galaxy was created.

The higher self is that instrument of translation that will always give you the answers, but they are answers you may not want to hear. Questions and answers are funny; they're like the chicken and the egg—the illusion of time. You can see it in your own mind, "I've got a question," and the moment that you congeal, "I've got a question," it's a linear question. Then the question goes like this. You've already heard the answer or you've already chosen the answer you want. If the answer doesn't come back echoing the answer you want, you become disoriented or you become angry.

We have to expand that identification of ourselves, and it's very difficult. On the one hand I'm saying to you, "Find out who you are, connect to your center." At the same time I'm saying, "Throw away your personal power, let it fall," because your way of attaining personal power has always been to your detriment. Move away from it, move away from "them vs. us." Focus your attention on that which is unmanifest and bring it into your physical vehicle. Take the responsibility of knowing that when you can manifest light, you can manifest matter. It is the same way a child is born, the same way a child is conceived. It is by recognizing that whole, that figure eight. The electrons move within the figure-eight pattern, and when they are released, they begin to spew. This is how the miracle procreated in the first place, and now we can allow ourselves to go back to the patterning. We can use the higher aspect of the mind to perceive it in that way, to perceive it in light, to perceive it as divine, and to perceive each other as divine.

If you move away from your positionality and really look into someone's face, you will see the pain, the struggle, the experience the individual has had in this lifetime or some other lifetime. You can awaken compassion that releases you from the judgment, from the self-righteousness of your positionality. That is the fluid that is moving through those limitations to an expanded octave.

People always have the idea that we have to struggle for something. We have to fast, pray, give up, be good in order to attain our higher self or to touch God. We must turn the dial to the frequency of the higher self. Once we become aware of the frequencies we're using, we can make a choice. If you feel what you feel like when you're angry, and you feel what you feel like when you're laughing, you'll see there's a tremendous difference of frequency. You have a choice; you can spin the dial. It is the same way with the higher self; it is the same way with the divine aspect. If you want to palpate it, it's always there with you.

Initiation is focusing your attention on the divine and holding the flicker in place for a long time, and it's hard for us. It's hard for us to stay in the divine consciousness in time and place. That's why we got into ritual, going into our caves, doing all those things so we don't collapse our attention. Now we need to drop those rituals. We need to drop the things that are in the way of understanding. You don't have to put the questions and answers in linear form. You can simply move to the energy and recognize it. The energy will push back. It's like a push in the air which we can perceive. If I focus my attention on that, I see what it is that's there. That's all we have to do. We don't have to struggle, we don't have to be perfect. Enlightenment is within us because the light is within us. We simply are much more comfortable in the darkness, in our hiding.

We don't have to do anything to perceive a part or aspect of our holograms, of our multidimensional selves. We simply have to surrender and say, "Guide me." That's all. There's nothing magical about it. The more we ask for it, the clearer it comes in. The more we will hear those answers from our higher selves, the better the translation becomes. We're able to perceive the whole so that we know when we're saying, "Shall I quit the job?" or "Shall I marry this person?" the answer is there and it's not yes or no, but it's *within*. All of us know each question has an increment of meaning, whereby the answer was within the question. It is an exquisite encapsulation.

When you look at the akashic records, at the records of all linear time, often what you see are little shapes that look like chromosomes. Some are L-shaped, some are curly, some are different colors, and those are the increments of meaning, of experience, of reality that we can then rub against to precipitate into an octave of understanding that we can get with our minds. But we have to come into our higher mind. If you're still hanging on to *you*, you're not going to get it. You're not going to hear it because your fear level is always going to say, "You see, I told you there's nobody out there."

You are your higher self. That's the cosmic joke. There are few teachers outside ourselves. The gurus are leaving this planet. They're physically lifting their bodies out, and they're doing that because it's *our* turn. You cannot demonstrate and manifest the power that is needed on this planet to clear radiation, conquer death, make choices, get rid of sickness, or come into harmony with other planets and other realities and other dimensionalities, until you can accept that the spiritual teacher is not outside yourself. It is within each one of you, and there are no excuses, and there are no handicaps. "I would if I could but I can't." No. People who are really stuck on that notion are going to leave. Watch.

It's a wonderful time. It's a thrilling time, and we need to palpate and touch it. It's there in you, in me, in all. You can make it as hard as you want. We're really into putting it out there just beyond reach or making sure we have to run somewhere else to get it, just to prove to ourselves that we're worthy. You're worthy! And you have all the knowing. You'll never, ever need anything but what's inside you. And what's inside you is unending because it is multidimensional.

When people release lifetime after lifetime, they will clear this theme, go all the way around the circle, and then they'll start on another theme and another theme. Pretty soon they stop living their lifetimes on this planet. They find themselves in some galactic position, some other planet, some other consciousness, dimension, and they let go, because they experience it multidimensionally. There's no end to this radiating consciousness we call the divine force. There's no end to us. It is simply the deliciousness of our choices, and we do need to learn to be delicious about it.

Our emotional bodies on this planet are stuck at a very low, slow-vibrating level. We must move up into those frequencies of exaltation—those high-pitched frequencies that are the frequencies of the divine, in which life and death spin, in which the material and immaterial spin. When we can attune to that, we can manifest the octaves, the birthright that these bodies have brought for us to manifest.

If you really entertain the possibility that you are multidimensional beings, you will recognize that there are no wrong choices. You don't have to clutch. You can't take the wrong road. You can simply make a choice that will teach you this lesson or that one, each of which will bring you back to your center. When we experience the freedom, when we experience the surrender with that understanding and release judgment so that we move into unconditional love, we are going to manifest everything, so that we can be who we truly are.

◇

TEN

THE HOLOGRAM

*When you have
trained your intentionality,
you will walk this Earth
as gods.*

Enlightenment is to be able to reach out into other octaves and other dimensions and pull in information that expands our capacity beyond the genius level. This is a very down-to-earth way to talk about our multidimensional selves. There are other dimensions, and there is information and energy, and there is access to those other dimensions that can nourish and heal us. In other words, we can begin to explain multidimensionality not as a science-fiction term, not as an esoteric term, but as a reality and a frontier. The mind is the frontier, but the mind exists beyond the limits of the brain. We can access through our consciousness other dimensions which can nourish us, which can amplify, which can teach us here and now in this plane. At The Light Institute, we want to help people to begin to contact their multidimensionality. We do that initially with past lives, because they are very immediate. As in the emotional-body session, through past-life sessions we can feel the energy, see the scenario, and recognize ourselves there. That's the first octave of the rippling out, of the extending pool of consciousness.

Of course, the second we expand who we think we are right now, we fall smack into past-life memories as well as other dimensional realities, because it's part of the coding that is in an identical infrastructure of our bodies.

You have to let go of all your little stuff. Rituals are going to take us back into the astral dimension, into the consciousness that you had at the time you began using the rituals. Our present-day rituals have become boring to us. They've lost their meaning. Also, because they're spoken in a language, our wonderful, finite minds start picking them apart. So we entice ourselves by chanting in another lanᵍuage. We like a little candlelight. That's great, because it triggers our attention. The second we surrender and focus our attention and our intentionality, we can go anywhere we want. It's irrelevant whether we go into a past life, another dimension, an expanded state of consciousness, into perceiving what is happening on the other side of the world, or into taking our bodies and bilocating them on the other side of the world. The training of intentionality activates holographic pulsations radiating from a synchronized brain center. It's important to understand that we are not talking about the "will" type of intentionality, but the intentional surrendering into the natural cycle of motion once inertia has been overcome. Since we live in a dimension where the brain is recording sights, sounds, and smells from the astral dimension, we need to clear those in the frequency of our brains. We need a frame of reference for that experience, because it is being within that frame of reference that allows us to advance.

If you went back to the child in you and said, "I can feel, I can put my hand on you and feel somebody," you might, depending on the balance of your karma, be able to just get up and do that. Likely as not, there will be something that's holding you back from actually manifesting it. The purpose of past-life work is clearing. It is to clear that energy, so the child within you can go to work and do that which you came here to do.

Just going back into your childhood is still a frame of reference in which there is an ego level. The ego is very purposeful for us. The ego is that which allows you to carry out your karma. "I'm so and so, that's why I'm here. This is who I am." And though it gets in our way 90 percent of the time, it keeps us in this dimension. You can recognize that there's day and there's night and there's danger. When we begin to clear, we free ourselves from limitation, and that allows us to manifest now.

I am into manifestation. That's what we're here for. When we go into a past life, we might find that, for example, in Atlantis, we were out there using our crystals and blowing it up. Today, everybody's out there using their crystals again. You may have been misusing your power before, but you had the power, which means you *still* have the power. It's only your guilt and judgment that's in the way of your using it. It's only your emotional body's attachment to saying, "I'm a victim," that is keeping you from manifesting in the first place.

When you go into a past life, you begin to perceive the way your soul has moved. It is an exquisite dance. You may have done your work in healing or music. Someone else may have done it in cognitive structuring of physical organisms like the mind. Your soul has a hologram for particular things. It's wonderful. It's "the best movie in town" to find out that "I don't have to do it in *this* kind of form," that "I can do it in *that* kind of form." It begins to open all kind of possibilities for you.

The more that each of us moves into the octave of understanding that the game "king of the mountain" doesn't work here, the more powerful we can be. If only parents and children understood that. If only the parent of a wild and bossy two-year-old understood that each of us needs to experience our power, and that the more you experience the power, the more you learn to refine it, and the more you're going to use it. So if you bungled this in Atlantis, you have an opportunity *now* not to bungle it. That's what we're about. We can each empower each other; the more powerful you are, the more powerful I can be.

What happens with the child is that the cognizance of that power is not verbal, is not in linear form. It may be in lights. It may be in flowers and rocks talking to you. But the challenge and the dictate of this time, for all souls, is to translate these right-brain experiences into the third dimension. When you go back into experiencing a past life, you're going to work with the brain functioning as an adult, saying, "Oh, this is what happened," or "Oh, this is cosmic death," or "I experienced that and then this happened," or "This is the reason for all of that." It's the *experiencing* that changes the molecular structure of the body. If you get it in your head, you're not doing much. It will help to some degree, but what you want to do is release it from your physical vehicle, free the physical vehicle.

Many times people come in with chronic diseases, and they discover that time after time they have focused their attention on a particular organ and have died this way over and over again. Nine out of the ten ways that they died were due to the heart or due to the throat or had to do with what's bothering them now. You know what happens? I don't want to say, "Do past-life work and get rid of your disease," but I want you to observe the hologram and understand that once you let go of what you're attached to, everything that's attached to it is gone too. It has to do with cognating through the dimensions, through all those frequencies. It's physical, it's mental, it's emotional,

145

it's spiritual.

Then people begin to experience other dimensions, relationships on other dimensions, and other realities that give them information that's useful to them now. Their subtle bodies are part of their informational systems. In other words, when we first move into the light body, the level of our consciousness at the light body level is nowhere. With the higher mind, it is the same thing. The mental body encompassing that higher mind is simply an expanded octave of consciousnessness that allows us to perceive. We're always filtering in through our six senses, but we're perceiving with a new sensitivity. We're always getting out there and drawing that experience in and translating it into this dimension.

A lot of times there's a warp in the translation. The more we do it, the less the warp. The warp comes in relationship to the density of our emotional bodies, our physical vehicles, our mental bodies. If our consciousness can't allow for the fact that there are other powers beyond these powers, other frequencies, or that things are not always in polarity—that two things that seem opposite can be the same—we go through a warp. That warp is called judgment and self-righteousness and constriction of the mind capacity, of the brain. But once we begin that conscious pool-expansion, then we can access that expansion, and the filter becomes clearer and clearer.

We find other ways to bring it through in a reality structure. That's why people so often say, "I don't know what you said, I don't know what happened. But I know. I can *feel* the difference." They often will literally *feel* the difference in the head, when the two lobes of the brain begin to pulsate in synch. They recognize it, and they can go back and access it again. We simply open the door, allow them to go through, and protect that passage.

The higher mind has the capacity to see the hologram, to perceive the truth, the consciousness, in an expanded way. The higher self issues forth from the soul, is the soul's blueprint coming forth. With the higher self and the higher mind, each one is the translator of the next, and so the higher mind helps to organize your consciousness of the higher self. The soul is divine. Then it moves into the higher self, which brings this profound hologram into a level where we can palpate it. The higher self is the descent into matter. If you looked at it that way, you'd see the soul, the higher self, the higher mind, and then the bodies.

The higher mind simply allows you to cognate on a higher octave. It allows you to work on a genius level in which the two halves of the brain function in synchronicity. The higher mind is really the genius level itself. The finite mind is a dot that represents linearity. The higher mind is a radiating circle around that, and it allows you to continue a ring higher and higher, which encompasses that first dot. The genius level is able to see the solution of the problem, because it sees the whole. It sees the roots, all the branches, the tree, the whole of it. It sees the hologram.

The blueprint of the soul is the dictate of the whole which says, "I will break off and go into experience in order to recognize the whole, the divine." When people go into soul experiences; they have no body. They are total light, they are everything, they are God; there is total oneness, there is no separation. That's where the soul is created. The soul becomes a concept of individuality. The second some aspect of the divine says, "Break away and experience," then the soul sets up a blueprint that says, "In order for you to recognize that you are not separate and you are whole, you will have these experiences." You will understand death, you will understand all of these themes, and then the blueprint begins to emerge. Each time that soul enters spirit, enters matter, and we experience imprints, it lays down the positionality out of which the emotional body is born. This is a difficult concept, because we don't have emotional bodies on all octaves, although we do have experience on all octaves. When you have a body without a nervous system like ours, you have a whole different frame of reference. That's why galactics and other entities sometimes have no emotional response, which is why many galactic beings are really out of balance here on Earth. Their frame of reference does not include an emotional body as we know it.

We are talking about matter within certain dimensions. In our dimension, matter has the emotional body, with its positionality, spiritual octave, etc., within it. When the emotional body recognizes itself within the light of the soul, it loses its positionality and heals its judgment. That's exactly the pattern that we're using in our work at the Institute. *We're helping people bring the emotional body back into contact with the soul's blueprint.* And then there is the great cosmic "Ah-ha" that goes on, when the emotional body understands, "Oh yes, I did." It experiences with the full extent of its understanding that it chose those experiences.

Intellectually, we only scratch the surface of these concepts, because we can't really understand what it is to choose. It is something we only recognize and cognate to small degrees. The second anything goes wrong in our lives, we automatically say, "I didn't choose that." But we did, and when we surrender our knowing, more of ourselves is in contact with the soul and the soul's blueprint. The trick is that as soon as we make that experiential contact on a soul level, we lose our judgment and move off the karmic wheel, because we don't have to do it any more. It's like the great master who is no longer involved in the "doing."

Recognize that descent into matter. That's why we talk, even in our dimension, about getting off the pleasure/pain syndrome. We can become so full of pleasure or pain that we become addicted to a horizontal plane of experience. At the Institute, we place great emphasis on the emotional body, so we can clear that emotional body, to quicken and function on an ecstatic level. When we do so, we're going to take another vertical leap.

The difference is that the ecstasy is not associated with a frame of reference, but the negative is associated with the whole collective karmic pool. We recognize anger because we experience it in all of our multi-lives. The higher self is latent—it is there within the emotional body, but it is the unmanifest part of the emotional body. In other words, when the emotional body begins to experience ecstasy and rapture, it quickens itself, and spins off the density of those lower emotions. All of that sorrow and weightiness begins to reach for its own knowing, and that's when it recognizes itself. When the emotional body truly recognizes itself, life and death and karmic cycles end.

The higher self permeates everything, but since it is unmanifest, we have to find the access point. It comes through these incredible vehicles as they move together, and as they are locked and butted up against each other. We create the window to the sky. We create that access, that bridge that allows us to palpate the higher self, so that the higher self does not even have to say "yes" in a linear way. The higher self has a different gyration. Another way to look at it is as a spiral, a spinning spiral, which is very different than a horizontal plane.

The reality of the multidimensional self is manifested through the hologram. We do not "reach" the hologram; we *are* the hologram. What happens is that we become fixated at different spots on the hologram, and we lose our understanding that there's something across the circle. We have no idea that we're connected to something across the circle, just as we have no idea that we can pull a string and tap the unconscious. We don't realize that we are in a fluid medium. We might call that the body, the universe; let us learn to call that the hologram.

In the hologram, we can recognize that we are here right now, and yet we have also lived many lives. We can experience and access the energy of those lifetimes, and that's the experiential aspect of the hologram. It is what the hologram really represents to us. It is not something out there to be tamed; it is simply that the more we become conscious of the hologram, the more we become God.

In a linear way, we cannot come to the place where we can manifest ashes, or manifest flowers, or stop an earthquake until we can perceive the hologram. Within creation there is destruction; we are a part of all that is, be it killer, lover, rain forest, or dead sea. As we open up to this great truth, we can heal ourselves through expansion. It is contraction—attention on the small, the incarceration of energy—which creates pain and suffering. The second we stop the cosmic flow and see the contents, we feel the chaos. We say, "This is discordant." But in fact, if we listen to the whole concert, nothing is in discord, because everything is within the latticework of our divine design.

We can learn to experience everything in the hologram funneling through this physical body, if we attune it to a harmonic interface with our subtle bodies. The clearer our physical, emotional, and mental bodies are, the more we can perceive the hologram. We can understand the connection to the God force, rather than having that perception, that concept that God is separate out there, or that anything else out there is separate.

At the Institute, we create a threshold for people to begin accessing the hologram, to recognize that anything they see or experience is a part of themselves. This is a concept that people initially cannot understand; they cannot grasp that there are no victims because they are locked within a positionality that says "This is who I am here." They are not experiencing their hologram. When they experience the hologram, they experience the whole connection.

Every time you experience yourself in another body, in another birth and death, in another relationship, you bring the hologram to its whole and access that whole. Even if you can perceive nothing but this lifetime, your present positionality, you are still the hologram, because it exists whether you perceive it or not.

All we are doing at the Institute is expanding our capacity to recognize the hologram. When people begin to experience that concept, it alters them because it heals separation. It's not, "I have to hurry up and be better. I've got to fix this thing, so I can have that over there." Instead, it's enlightenment. Enlightenment knows that perfection is being in the center of it all. That's the first octave of enlightenment—holding the flicker into the flame, so that we can be in the midst of whatever that chaos is, and always feel ourselves inside the cosmic giggle.

It is a wonderful experience in relationships just to find yourself yelling or being angry, and at the same time, the giggle is going on because you know that it is just you playing. It happens simultaneously. It's not the mind saying, "Oh, you know that this isn't who you really are." At the same time that you're starting to shout, there's this tremendous giggle, because you're experiencing the humor of this part of your posturing.

Once we begin to have those kind of experiences, our attachment to the anger or to the self-righteousness or to the positionality is simply erased. The same time that you're in the midst of crying, the cosmic giggle that is bubbling up, because you know you're just performing for yourself. You can begin to forgive the performance and say, "No, I don't really have to do this." Just as you do with the two-year-old, you simply switch the body onto something else.

When we come into those places of dissolution, and we can't fix it and its going to be deadly, etc., all we need to do is to come around to contact on the soul level, within the hologram of that entity, outside of that arena and posture. That's what is so beautiful about past-life work. It allows us to do that. It allows us a frame of reference certainly for those with whom we've been sons and lovers and friends. We've known them before, so we can pick and choose how we're seeing them right now.

If a part of somebody is falling off the ledge, you can say, "Let me experience you on a soul level." And you can embrace that. And the second you consciously choose to reach in on that soul level, your tears will stop, because you'll know it's useless. If someone wants to die as an alcoholic or as a victim, it's OK, because all of that person isn't there. There's all the rest of their hologram. You can, through your conscious will, through your intentionality, merge with another part of them. That is called holding the flicker to the flame. What I'm talking about is creating reality. That is the experience of, or the translation of, what we mean when we say: "Let go."

How do you let go? The way you let go is by expanding your consciousness. That's the only way to let go. When the consciousness expands and you experience people on a soul level, perhaps even a different memory of them, what will happen is the emotional body will lift up. The tears stop, the emotional body starts to breathe, starts to radiate out, and you make contact. The second you do that you are creating another reality, a reality of compassion.

Our children will not deal with themselves in our old ways. There will be very little residue of that. They'll be able to access the highest octave very quickly. This is the planet of the heart chakra, so we must have emotion, we must feel the heart, we must understand separation and merging. At this point, we are barely flickering the concept of merging. It is a totally foreign concept to us. When we come to that octave, the emotional body will not be as we know it today. When we clear our past lives, we are clearing them forever. We are erasing history! The soul is thus able to move into octaves for which we have no frame of reference yet.

"Try" is a word we never use, because "try" is always the struggle of resistance, the swimming upstream. It is always the Doubting Thomas who says, "I don't know if I can." We *will* do it. And it's not out there. It's simply recognizing it, expanding into it. All we are doing is *pushing the envelope*. Your emotional content will come up whether you like it or not, whether you're trying to hold it down, whatever you're doing with it. The best thing is to simply honor that.

There may be places where you're in the most defunct space, where you're the opposite of your ecstasy, because once the pendulum starts moving up to new octaves, it creates a tremendous swing back and forth. It is just teaching you. But each time, it swings back a little less and goes up a little higher. The reason for that is you're not pulling so hard to the low side any more. The emotional body isn't quite so insistent on getting into anger and fury, because it is getting interested in what's over here on the high side. It is starting to palpate new frequencies. There is no seduction in what's going on up here, so initially, there is the attempt by the ego self, by the emotional body, to entrap you. I call that "initiation," and all you have to do is recognize it. The second you get a clearing, you feel profound love, and the very first person that comes around you is going to try to test you on that. That individual is going to try to stimuate your fear or your separation or your judgment. That person is a test of who you are, and we say, *let go.* When you meet that person, merge with that being, let that person see who you really are, then you will find ecstasy, the new frequency.

◇

ELEVEN

DEATH AND
SAMADHI

*Unspeakable guilt and judgment
lock you into the body
so that you repeat the body,
so that you wear only the body
and not the light which is
your true frequency.*

Karin had begun driving at about twelve years old around our tiny town.
I wanted to be sure that when she hit the highways, she would not be an inex-
perienced driver. She was fourteen now and though she mostly drove her father's
truck, I felt totally comfortable watching her behind the wheel of our huge Dodge
Maxi-Van. It was late afternoon as we headed down the Lamy hill toward
home. We were in the middle of a heated political discussion, when suddenly
she lost control of the van while negotiating a curve. We began veering off the
highway. A voice inside me shouted for her to take her hands off the wheel,
warning that otherwise we would be killed. Time stopped while I considered
that blood-chilling possibility. Then the van swerved and I was thrown behind
the driver's seat. I remember the voice commanding me to go limp. It was as
if I were a rag doll being thrown from ceiling to floor with arms and legs in a
cartwheel position. I concentrated on going limp and there was even a bizarre
thought that this was rather fun. After four rolls the van came to a stop up in
the air with its nose buried in the ground. Several drivers following us down the
hill stopped and pulled us out and onto the ground. What followed was one
of the most amazing demonstrations of multi-dimensional consciousness I have
ever experienced.

As we lay stretched out on our backs, we reached to touch our fingers
together. Karin was sobbing and pleading for me not to die. I told her not to be
afraid, to let me go, as I felt a tremendous urge to rise up out of my body. I was
literally pushing from the inside out. Meanwhile, I saw a man standing there
and I could see that in his compassion he was extending very healing energy

153

streams toward me. I asked him to place his hand over the left side of my head. A policeman had arrived on the scene and in the most lucid manner I instructed him to convey specific instructions to the hospital—that I refused medication, surgery, etc.—and I gave him five names and telephone numbers of people to be notified immediately.

Simultaneous to all of this, my awareness took me into two unforgettable, other-dimensional experiences.

As I surged upward from my body lying on the ground, I came to some kind of interface wherein I was met—or, I should say, stopped—by a group of energy beings. Much to my horror, they did not seem to be radiant beings of light coming to welcome me, but rather they felt more like dark clouds menacing toward me, resisting my gesture to enter. As I persisted, they became more and even more aggressive, almost angry. Suddenly the presence of a young woman who had stayed in my house while I was away in Bolivia, and who had died the year before in a tragic car accident, moved to the front and pushed toward me. As she did so, they all shouted in unison: "Go back; you can't come here! You can't come now!" I was so stunned that I fell back into my being, confused and lost. Where was the heavenly, loving reception we had always heard of, I asked myself. I can only tell you that this was one of the bleakest moments of my present existence.

Then I suddenly became aware of a sense of motion, which felt like a floating, rising sensation. Several translucent, rainbow-colored globes of light appeared. I was within their sphere of radiance and received transmissions—at what seemed the speed of light—relating to the source, meaning, and laws pertaining to all of life. Every particle of my multi-dimensional soul was caressed and nourished. I was bathed in bliss.

Three weeks went by before my hair unraveled from its centrifugal spin. It actually stood out from my head in tight ringlets. People kept fretting over the way I looked. They insisted that I was still in shock. I appeared transparent; my eyes had a shiny, almost disturbing stare to them; and my face was radiant. It would startle me when I looked in the mirror, because of the depth of the energy staring back at me, but I knew what it was and I always will. Next time I move to the threshold, my timing will be perfect.

Our essential lesson here on Earth is to experience, to embrace death and *samadhi*. Two energies entwined, interlocked, dancing together, inseparable. One flowing into the other, the other flowing back again. We are here to palpate from this side of the veil what it is to have the capacity to move through the channel of death to the unmanifest, to that which is our true being, to that which is the divine, universal frequency, which is all-knowing, which is samadhi. Enlightenment.

Enlightenment comes only to the thrust, to the passage back. And that is the gift of death. Death is not a dark energy. Death is not in opposition to life. Death is simply a leaving. When we embrace our body, when we are held in the profound clutch of our emotional body, we are unable to spring forth into that light which is the actuality of our being in unmanifest form. We come into body, and we take on the aspects, the juice of this emotional body which is imprinted with every experience of life. The imprint which passes from body to body is what creates the downward spiral of fear which separates us from being able to embrace death from the position of mastery.

What lingers with us then is attachment to experience, that drinking-in of the emotional frequency of fear. It keeps us from palpating, from utilizing experientially, the gift which is death. Death is only a passage, a surrendering, which guides us forth into the expansion, into that expanding swirl which is our true self without encumberment. And so we linger. We linger in our life, in our denial, in our fear, and we become obsessed, we become our fear. As we crystallize into that fear, we lose our life. We lose the purpose, the blueprint of our choice, which is to come here and move within the dance. The fear ripples out from us, and we find that we cannot love, we cannot move, and we cannot speak the heart because we have created this material, physical imprint which separates us from our true being, from the whisper of our multidimensional, never dying, divine self.

Death is the tearing away, the breaking away from that which we are involved in now. We create for ourselves lives of resistance—resistance to the capacity of our gift. And so we repeat karma, we repeat the pulsation, each time changing a bit, but always within the theme, the frequency of that to which we are attached. We do not allow the soul to expand its searching. But, its choice in moving into body was to expand itself. The divine grows through this dimension, through our incarnation, through our physical selves as the ripple of the God-nature expands. The sensation which is just on the other side of that tunnel of death is ecstatic, is freedom. It is samadhi.

To move and to work with the energy of death, we have to

quicken the time. We have to quicken the degree of stuckness in the tunnel to the rushing forward of that which is called home. The choice of passing back and forth, back and forth, which is the inevitable pulsation of the universe between manifest and unmanifest, can be done directly, without resistance, without the break. The gift that is given to all of us encountering this work is to come again and again to that moment of death, so that we can recognize and release from ourselves our history. We can move into a place of no time, a place of the ever-now, the ever-present. Each time we embrace a lifetime and we recognize ourselves there, we can speak to the molecular structure of this vehicle and allow it to let go of that history.

The history that our bodies have experienced creates the addiction, creates the fear that attracts us to this side rather than the other side—which is separated by such a thin membrane of reality. It is a great gift to experience these multiple-life experiences, if for no other purpose than embracing the recognition of the death. That is why at the Institute we are so interested in that moment in each session—of the choice that you create in that passing. Unspeakable guilt and judgment lock you into the body so that you repeat the body, so that you wear only the body and not the light which is your true frequency.

Each time you see a death that you acknowledge as your own, you have a moment of great wisdom. If you stop there in that choosing, you can expand, cross that membrane into samadhi, which is the knowing which recognizes the perfection of that choice. If you were to play it again, you would see that there was nothing left but death in that lifetime. There was nothing left there for you, no increment of living left for you, and so you were free to go. It is only the imprint of your emotional body that decides the dance of that death and dying—whether you are violent with yourself, whether you have the mastery to seduce some other soul to be violent with you, or whether that passing is one of great knowing, of great light.

The body carries the brunt of the spirit. When we look at a body, we can know the story of the spirit. The spirit is on this side of the veil of manifestation, and it holds the knowing, it holds the choosing, it holds the denial. The spirit holds all of the imprints of the emotional body, so as we peel away death and look again and again at the choice of the dying and the drama of our passing—we know the essence. We go on and on through our deaths, and eventually what happens is that we come to the dying which is of grace. We come to the releasing, to the letting go of the task, the dance, the school. Welcome to this side of the veil!

Then we are able to pull through the samadhi, the knowing, into this side. We can draw the ecstasy into this side, into manifestation. Then consciousness registers *"I'm finished; there is no more for me; I can slip through. I can slip through effortlessly."* When you come to a dying in which you have done that, a dying in which you have laid down the body with grace, blessing, and love for the gift that it gave you, for the gift that it gave your divine soul—then you are forever after a master!

At any moment, the molecular structure of these bodies that we are carrying right now can be altered. At any moment, we can let go of the resistance enough to draw light in, so that we can live fully—which is our birthright. Our birthright is to walk through the wall, to raise the dead. It is to recognize the choice of any soul—whether it be a starving being or a small child or a beloved parent. It is to have the power, to have the wisdom to make its choice to live or die with grace.

Of course, the difficulty within our bodies is that our emotional bodies not only become attached to our sins, but we become attached to each other. We have a lot of difficulty in that passage of death and letting go. The focus of our consciousness is in the dying and not in the ecstasy—not in the expansion and freedom of releasing. The energy that is created at the moment of death is so profound. If you fear death, then go and stand at the side of someone dying, and you will experience something incredible. The universe never wastes energy. There is never a movement, a thought, a choice that is not for the highest good. There is no waste; it is impossible within cosmic law. When you are there in the presence of death, there is that moving forth from this focus across the veil to the other side. There is a tremendous charge of energy, as all the electromagnetic energy is released from holding, from the coalescing. There is a letting go of messages of the soul's choice, of the soul's teaching, a rush into that expanded state that goes on and ripples on and on and merges and touches and is never alone again.

It is an incredible experience to witness death, because it is a moment of releasing. Our fear is always about the body's memories. It is a profound gift to move into experience of multiple lifetimes, to view the hologram of the akashic record, which is the record of our experience here. If we release our history, then it is within the molecular structure of this choice, of this coalescence, that we can choose only light, grace, and consciousness. When people move away from their experience here at the Institute, and they move to their own karma and their everyday world, they can carry that seed of knowing that allows them to be totally free.

How can you be afraid of someone else's judgment when you've died and come again? When you recognize with incredible joy that each soul has choice, you will see that each soul chooses to be the victim, chooses to be the victimizer, chooses to stay, or chooses to leave. How can it be? If you can turn that flicker of consciousness into a flame and take that into your daily life, then would you be afraid of disapproval or flinch at a parent's comment? You would not, because the child within you would always step forward to the adventure of life. Recognize that when we merge the body with the light—death and samadhi—we become totally free. We know our emotional body never chooses that death, because it is afraid that it will not hear the echo of its name any longer. It is invested in its existence. What if all the lives, all the beings, were not spoken, were not heard?

At the Institute, we teach people to exercise the stillness, to focus on being taught during sessions by their higher selves. With that focus, they know beyond a shadow of a doubt that the cells in their bodies are dying all the time. Every cell in our body dies within a seven-year cycle; there is the coming and the going constantly. We exist at the level of our focus; the ego can let go. We must step forward, we must ripple out.

We have found in our work that the child in us is always ready, because the child is not locked into the focus of constriction of the karma of this body. Even the auric field of a child sparkles and spews and sputters. It is not coalesced, and so it can rush off to the unmanifest at any moment. Its brain can pulsate in an alpha frequency that allows it to contact its multidimensional self—other kingdoms, other consciousnesses—that allows it to let go of that clasping fear of the emotional body's memory that says, "Look out! Look out! I won't *be* any more." We will always *be*. We have always *been*. We will die and die and die, and we will be born and be born and be born.

It's how long we've danced within that karma that we carry in the funnel of death that triggers the fear. We can pass instantly, or we can do it over and over again in our life. If we are afraid of the finality, practice the *now*. This is what I'm talking about when we look at our other lives, when we experience our deaths.

Why do so many people come to the Institute for this work? The gift that they get in these experiences can radiate from them to everyone within their karmic pool. As they become peaceful with death and samadhi, they can say to the ego, "It's all right to let go of the two-year-old; it's all right to let go of the rebellious teenager." It's all right to let go of the denial and to experience that crossing-over constantly in your life; that pulsation exists in every octave of your reality. The degree to which you can let go is the degree to which you can experience samadhi, or knowing.

The discharge of death in the physical body, the discharge of anything that we are holding, creates ecstasy whether it is in the mind or in the emotions or in the physical body. It does. It's the gift given for releasing. It is the movement which is cosmic law. All things are constantly moving. The trick is to teach this to the emotional body, which holds us within the constraints of this vehicle, the constraints of our relationships, the constraints of our minds. The trick is to simply jump across the abyss. We must become that which leaps forward—the child that jumps forward to meet reality, to meet life.

We cannot perform as masters in this dimension until we have embraced death. The universe is not just creation; it would get very crowded with just creation. There is the creation and there is the disassociation and there is the creation, just like the DNA, always moving in and out. To be a master in this lifetime is the purpose for which each and every one of us has come. This is a pivotal moment in the choice of our collective souls. We have come here to give our gifts. We have come here to release all of the knowing. You cannot release the knowing while you are holding the stuff of the emotional body, because it creates the cloud, the confusion, and the positionality that says, "I am here and I am right and I am it." And that is very lonely. And so we must now move to that capacity to release the master that is in each and every one of us, that is waiting to be born within the conscious aspect of our reality.

We have to reach across the veil. We have to move back into the unmanifest and pull in and precipitate that knowing, that recognition, that allows us to let go. One does not happen without the other. The yin does not live without the yang, which does not live without the yin. The pulsation within the body, within the cells—catabolic, anabolic, catabolic, anabolic—is constantly pulsating. Death is that space in between that cannot see in either direction.

We must now clear, quicken, educate, and embrace our emotional bodies so that they can make that leap and let the self go. Whether that is on a cellular level or an emotional level, personality level, or higher level of consciousness, it makes no difference. We can see ourselves in our limitations, we can see ourselves in the blackness of death, or we can see ourselves in the hologram that laughs. We must become light. That is the gift of samadhi. That is the gift of death. Because it's a great laugh to die and find yourself still laughing! And that's exactly what happens. The consciousness leaps through, and there you are again. And there you are again.

You must seek those experiences that put you in the face of death. Whether it is the death of the little ego—"I cannot perform this task." You can die! What task is there that you cannot perform? You must embrace each time you come to the moment of death. And to teach yourselves that, you can give space for that in your lives. You can tune your attention in to listen within this physical vehicle. That is the greatest gift of the soul, because it is allowing for its evolution of the soul by allowing experience. You can listen within the vehicle to the dying of the cells. And you can listen and embrace and recognize that process everywhere. You can do that with great lightness. With great humor. And you can put yourself in the path of that process to test it so that you become strong enough to live. After you've heard the dying of cells, you'll be ready to hear the sound of cells birthing. It's a divine hum!

I have passed across the channel of death four times. I have held dying babies in my arms. I have rubbed up against the smell of death and the sight of death. I have become so unsacred as to be able to smile, because I have allowed my consciousness to move across that veil and simply pluck myself to the other side. We are all going to be profoundly involved in that very process because it is part of our mastery. When someone you know dies—or someone you think you don't know, but you do dies—if you will take your consciousness to this octave above fear, to the octave of the child that says, "Let me truly know. Let me merge with you, and then I will know," you will experience that reality, that profound wisdom of the choice of every being who moves to the initiation of death. Because death is the initiation of life. And we must begin to practice it, and we must begin to use it.

People are dying all around us. All we need to do is to move out from our personal karma, from the encapsulation of that thought-form that says, "I am separate," and allow the conscious stream to move to the target, whether that's a cell or a lover or a stranger. Make contact with the experience. You will have a profound revelation of ecstasy as you allow your energetic system to come into contact with the releasing. You can help in this passage that is going on around this global environment which we have chosen together, you and I, to release that energy, to recognize that you can participate in the plucking, participate in the releasing of the energy that allows one being to arrive. Arriving is samadhi, because it is the recognition, it is the knowing. It is past that place of resistance. That is mastery.

We can palpate and stimulate it. We can radiate it in our own personal lives so that every one around us who is in a state of fear can sense the quickening that has happened to us. Sense it in our presence, and on some octave of their own being, make contact, be encouraged to let go. To know that the letting go here is the welcoming there. Let us practice this now, because there is great death going on at this moment, not only within our individual cells, but within our human family. And we are being profoundly asked to release that coagulation within the funnel that is causing beings to be locked in the astral dimension.

If we die in a way in which the emotional body is not brought forward as well, is left there lingering in confusion or self-righteousness or positionality or judgment or vengeance, then the process is not complete. So we only move one ripple from our physical vehicle, only to that frequency of the astral. The astral body and the astral dimension have weight, have matter, have stick-em. They entrap us in the karmic pool and return us again to bodies. Our astral dimension at this time is becoming so polluted because the quantity of bodies leaving this world in a state of confusion, positionality and vengeance, is beginning to literally smother us. The Earth too is smothering. It is getting ready to shed itself, to shudder, in order to cause a release, because the tension is building up so much. We need to become conscious of that so that we can change our destiny at this point.

Because we are turning away from death in every way in our culture, it is calling to us. This is a great gift that is forcing us back around to face death so that we can face our lives, face our mastery, which is the choice of our being born at this time. The density that is going on in the astral dimension is affecting the planet that we're living on. All of the prophecies that have been given for this time are unfolding even now as a gift to awaken us, so that we can recognize that if we could be here, free, unattached to our positionality, we could raise the dead, or we could stop an earthquake, or we could clear atomic waste. We could dance our lives fully.

We could profoundly relieve this confusion, and prevent and alleviate the suffering which will ensue as a result of this astral smothering, by lending our consciousness to clear the astral dimension of the spirits stuck within it.

What you can do now is move into the astral octave and draw those trapped energies up into the great light, so that they can move into their essence which is without form. Here is the exercise: Draw the light frequency in through the top of your head, and extend it out through your solar plexus. Pull the light in and extend it out through your solar plexus so that your auric field moves farther and farther out, so that you become part of the movement of that energy, that light in and light out. Identify yourself with that movement, with the light force.

Ask your higher self to locate the spirit of a person or groups of people you wish to help lift our of the astral dimension. When you feel yourself make the contact with their energy, simply begin by beaming love to them. Since the color pink carries the frequency of love, pink is a good color to use. Draw it into you and extend it out through your heart. When the communication is flowing, you may need to explain to them that they are entrapped and must continue on into the light.

Now begin to amplify the light so that it creates an illuminated highway of white light stretching up into the heavens. Urge them to think of their loved ones awaiting them and beam them up onto the transcending path into the light. For many souls, it is tremendously helpful to remember their emotional connections on the "other" side. It is their negative emotional connections which are keeping them on this side. Simply ask them to image their families and tell them to go home to them.

Sometimes the people they are going home to may be ones that they knew in a different lifetime, that you are not connected to. Their consciousness, their emotional energy, needs to focus on a recognizable energy because the fear is so great.

Notice now, that within your molecular structure you can experience the electricity of that release. Allow yourself to cognate that electrical, orgasmic frequency. As you do that, through your knowing and your grace, draw the light in through yourself and extend it outward, dispersing that grace. Then create again the vertical highway of white light that begins to move the energy up. Simply continue extending up and out until you do not encounter any resistance. Again, wait until you feel that electrical stimulus, then draw light into your own being, allowing yourself to radiate out. Radiate your light onto that ethereal octave of light that connects everything. You will know when this has occurred because there will be an overpowering sense of joy and lightness. You will feel a spacial clearing around you, like the difference between heavy clouds and blue sky

All of you have experienced other dimensions that offer us even more enrichment, even more deliciousness than this one, this physical one. We need to focus our consciousness to participate in that lifting of the astral dimension so that those beings can go on, so that we can go on. We can begin now to exercise that capacity. Because, of course, that is why you are here. More and more we will be called upon to radiate that which is true: to speak the heart, to live the knowing, to be the samadhi, to be the master.

◇

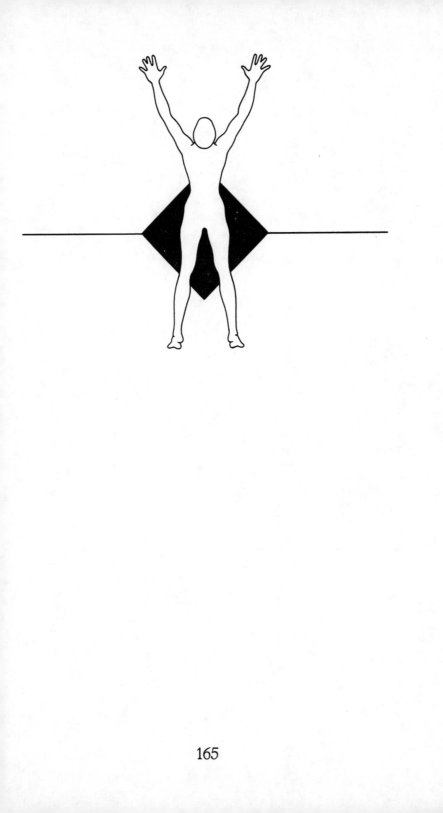

◇TWELVE◇
ECSTASY IS
A NEW FREQUENCY

*It is only when we have
dissolved enough to experience
ourselves as sound and light
that we can ride the currents of
ecstatic vibration.*

Ecstasy, as a word, creates within its sound a sensation of vibration, movement rising and falling, concavity, and scooping out. As it swirls, ecstasy creates an image, a sensation of high flutter. It is a flutter that undulates outward and remains unrooted in our everyday realities—a flutter which has no strings attached to the mind.

The anatomy of ecstasy is related to sound, to a high-pitched staccato vibration that energetically gives a sensation of fast, quick movement. Ecstasy moves through the passages of this vibration most easily to undulating currents of sound and light. It is only when we have dissolved enough to experience ourselves as sound and light that we can ride the currents of ecstatic vibration.

There are many octaves of ecstasy related to frequencies of consciousness. At first, ecstatic response is *electrical*. We can use the electrical systems of energy passages within our physical vehicle as well as within our subtle bodies to bridge our consciousness into ecstatic realms. To do this, we need only to allow the attention itself to merge into that electrical frequency. We become the electrical charge as it passes along the synapse and rushes through the chakras and body meridians, creating the fission which explodes and awakens the 72,000 nadis of the body.

Ecstasy is created when consciousness coalesces itself, when it swirls into form, and all the particles and subparticles bombard each other. With the friction, due to the proximity of particles to each other, the exploding creative force rushes out, creating and carrying light, releasing ecstatic energy. The interface between the ecstatic experiences and our human reality is where we find the electrical charge, the awareness. As we deliberately relay our attention on the sensational electrical quality of our entire physical system, it begins to climb the ladder, begins to move light higher along the frequency-grid, creating, as if by combustion, more and more energy. Within the electrical quality in nature, there is a cycle of ecstatic frequency that moves along the waves of universal pulsation. These are the peaks and valleys which delineate the quality of ecstatic frequencies.

Ecstasy begins with a heightened energy which is attuned to the emotional body. That energy is *rapture*; rapture occurs when the attention binds itself within a coalescent being. It is a heightened state of tension and can be likened to the inhalation of the divine breath, the prana, when the consciousness experiences itself in relationship to that prana, to the nourishment of that life-force energy. There is a sucking in and holding of energy, which is followed and accompanied by a great exhaling "haaa," which is bliss. Bliss is the valley—the pleasing, satisfying energy of exhalation which lets itself melt and flow out. When bliss and rapture begin their union, their divine pulsation, they rush in and out, creating a charge just as does conception. This marriage of bliss and rapture creates ecstasy.

Ecstasy soars upward, fueled by its own momentum, by its very being, transcending until it becomes an energy without a source. It becomes the source itself. This is the source which creates the worlds, creates the coalescence into thought, light, and form. This is the source which creates supernovas. Then it extinguishes itself to begin again after another cessation. It is the swelling moment of rapture, rewarded with bliss, exploded into ecstasy over and over again. It is the sourcing creative force across the entire universe. We use the nuances of these words in relationship to each other to explore the ecstatic frequency, which is itself a force field of divine energy in which we can learn to bathe our consciousness, to anchor our reality, to choose our path. The source ripples out in all directions on the current of ecstasy which knows no limitations or separations.

Since our own creation issues forth from the creative source, it is, then, a whisper of a structural component encompassing the cellular mind. Yet, it is a structural component that remains latent within the realm of possible compositions. Through some intervening consciousness, this component was shaken loose and allowed to begin a frequency which, having become manifest, having totally awakened, alters the composition of the whole. That is why we must seek the new energy, the new frequency, because one ecstatic being creates a ripple which sources unimaginable new realities—co-creation with the universe.

The mind cannot bring this energetic to flower. It is a surge, a quickening of our frequencies, which must advance us to within range of this evolutionary possibility. Our collective consciousness has been slow to respond to the echo of singular, ecstatic experiences obtained so rarely by beings who often shut themselves away from the interface of everyday human sharing. These few ecstatic saints, holy beings, have attained this frequency by separating themselves from any worldly distraction, but they have produced a whisper which has been heard and perceived through the collective latticework of other consciousness. Let us attune our frequencies so that we can begin to mimic the pulsating formulae of ecstasy. This frequency, with its unlimited divine potential, can create an evolutionary mutation of our physical, emotional, and mental bodies, so that we become ecstatic light bodies of consciousness!

The ecstatic frequency placed within the medium of a human body automatically transmutes any density of imprisoned energy. Ecstasy is not a goal to be achieved through some system of denial, or under some rule whereby we project outward to a vague future point along a continuum of unachieved reality.

Ecstasy is seeded within the source components of our cellular mind. Thus, we need to allow this great cretaceous encapsulation we've created around us by isolating into the third dimension, to collapse upon itself. We are to allow this shell to return to its fluid state of unconstricted potential. In order to find ourselves within the rapture, within the ecstatic frequencies, we must release our attention on our physical, linear constructs of being born, living, and ultimately dying, of allowing only that definition of our experience in time. We simply must divest ourselves of all pre-organized thought and turn our attention onto the light particles which use the frequency of light. This energy is intrinsic to us, and through it we can rediscover our divine source. We can take ourselves over and over again into that octave, however short-termed our capacity to stir within its ecstatic frequency.

During longer and longer periods of time we can become ecstatic consciousness itself, by simply returning to its indelible, albeit distant, memory. We can bring it forth. If we desire ecstasy, ours could become a continual ecstatic reality.

We can approach this by steps. The first step is learning to experience the electricity created within our own bodies. We can literally place our attention on the electricity generated within the cells of our bodies, our energetic meridians, as well as within the flow of the chakric system. We can use energies which allow us to explode out of our daily patternings into higher frequencies, such as becoming music or becoming light. We can do it by merging into the orgasmic and becoming the sexual pulsation ourselves. As we cease to hold ourselves in form with the linear model of the ego, we broaden the arc of consciousness. As we expand perception to any point in the universe, into any of our myriad, multidimensional realities, the ecstatic state is accessible to us. We become ecstatic as our energy is freed; we become ecstatic when we release a blockage within our emotional patterning. Any imprisonment within our consciousness that we let go of, whether it is physical, mental, or emotional, produces the quickening that allows ecstasy to gain a foothold.

Once the electrical charge has passed through the synapses, chakras, and nadis of the body, an awareness of conscious coalescence begins. We have an ecstatic experience, and we become the child again, which intensely reinforces the new response within our frequency-grid.

We can use experience as points of passage, as thresholds into ecstatic states. All it necessitates is the choice of consciousness. Once having experienced an ecstatic moment, we can always return to it, not necessarily by remembering the experience that precipitated the ecstatic frequency, but by laser-beaming our attention into the frequency itself, which is forever recorded once experienced. Moving into the consciousness of the cellular mind is a good place to begin to loosen the constriction of our self-image, because when we listen to the energy of the cell, to the electrons spinning and whirring within the cell, we automatically quicken. The body is the organization place of our cellular consciousness, and we can experience ecstatic states while being encompassed within our name and body.

When we contact the higher self, we immediately come into

ecstatic realms, and we can begin the interface between our present name and body and our multidimensional, unlimited, divine expression. Ecstasy is the higher self in action, the dance of the higher self within our being, the union. The presence of the higher self is always ecstatic if we hold our attention on that frequency. Ecstasy cannot be attained through struggle or discipline or self-righteousness. It can only be attained through surrender—surrender to effortless, divine pulsation. We simply must go back into our origins, into the conception, to merge with the ecstatic God force which created us.

The intense expansion of the ecstatic moment is often followed by an abrupt snapping-shut of the "windows to the sky." The new self suddenly experiences a profound feeling of nakedness. Stripped of all the old identities, it utterly reverses itself by charging backwards into the familiar, seductive darkness. This turn of events is met with approval and relief by those around us, who, after all, cannot continue to maintain their emotional patterns if we suddenly abandon our supportive roles in their movies. We, in turn, cling desperately to the illusion that we can "un-grow" ourselves back to what we were before. If we could watch this predicament from a space outside us, we would come upon the "cosmic giggle." Unbeknownst to us, we have already leapt off the precipice, and all our desperate gyrations in the attempt to scramble back up the ledge are utterly useless.

Seduction works only as long as it is unconscious. The moment we have pulled away the veil, we irretrievably extricate ourselves from its enticement. There is nothing more empty than enacting a passion or reality in which we no longer believe. We think we are powerless to go on, yet the hope of continuing the way we were disappears, erasing the steps behind us until we find ourselves again at the precipice.

Thus, surrender comes without thought, and we find ourselves falling, falling—without light, without before or after or beyond. We don't look back. We can't. We don't care any more. At this wondrous moment, the universe gives us the gift of the cosmic giggle. We discover that although we are falling, there is no bottom! This is samadhi, the cosmic joke. The energy transcends, and the hologram reorganizes itself. The emotional body has disintegrated and then quickened. We begin rising on the energy of the vertical axis. Light creeps in. It is the dawn of our consciousness. We know! Now we must look up and anchor the sky. We are radiant beings, newly born.

When the hum of ecstasy interpenetrates life-force energy, there is a spontaneous convergence of light from which springs the highest octave of divine play within manifest dimensions. It is the energy of radiance. Radiance is the result of the ecstatic spark which, once ignited, spreads itself out in all directions across the entire spectrum of manifest dimensions, out into the black void of the formless. The energy of radiance cannot be stopped or resisted or even engaged. When it bathes the path, all fear instantaneously metamorphoses into light. All separation, confusion, and longing cease to exist. Radiance moves beyond the electrical, the magnetic laws of the third dimension. It seeks to attract nothing, and nothing sticks to it. It merely pervades all.

In our clouded veil of linear existence, we have lost the awareness of ourselves as radiant beings. Yet that is what we truly are. We don't have to wait for some miracle to lift us up from the debacle of our negative emotional bodies. We can practice radiance within the framework of our present realities—right now.

Close your eyes, and begin breathing in the prana around you. With your eyes still closed, step to the center of your space—wherever it is. Standing there in the middle, begin the initial exercise of drawing in energy and radiating out through the solar plexus. Simply envision radiance moving effortlessly forth, filling all the spaces around you and traveling out into limitless space. You can expand out with the radiance, or simply extend it and let it go. It is like blowing dandelions to the wind.

We do not need to indulge ourselves in dilemmas of worthlessness; we only need to move to the choice. The more we practice radiance in our lives, the more we will become it. This is our evolution back into light. The attendant experience of rapture, bliss, and ecstasy are our birthright, if we will only agree to be born.

I was leaning forward onto my daughter's shoulder as the sun slipped behind the hill. I was in a state of heightened awareness. My consciousness seemed to be bursting with fascinating bits of information which I took in on several levels, even as my body was washed with wave after wave of seemingly incessant contractions. After the sun's piercing brilliance, the light now was a comforting glow. I felt that the air particles themselves were impregnated with life, and they seemed to be crowding around me, whispering encouragement.

The crystalline aqua sea and I were in intimate union with each other! I was within the sea, and it was within me. The light dancing on the water helped me focus my attention, and as I pushed in the waist-deep water, and into the light, it seemed to rejuvenate me. The sensation of the gently lapping water caressing my body offered me a kind of solace I had never felt before during labor.

Magically, a tiny hand emerged. A part of my consciousness rejoiced in my choice of a water birth, for I knew it would give me great help. I leaned forward in my weightless medium and he slid out, flowing backward between my legs into the hands of his father. As his nose touched the surface of the water, he took a deep breath and cried out to life. We passed him down under my legs again, like a little fish, and into my arms. His being took my breath away. Though he was past term, he was completely covered with white vernix. His transparency in the water gave him a luminous quality—silvery, bluish-white. As I submerged him back into the water, he opened his eyes and stared gently at me. The way his gaze held mine pierced my very soul—unfathomable, all-knowing, totally loving. Consciousness gave way, and I was swept up into an ecstatic rapture for which I will never have words, yet its frequency will seed my being forever.

The others had left us on the beach while they prepared for our homecoming. My son Britt and I, with the new being in my arms, sat on a blanket facing the sea. The late afternoon sun, as if to honor the birth, slipped reverently into the reflective water. The air and the sea sparkled and danced. It seemed as if the light passed through my eyes and undulated out in every direction, like heat waves rising off summer land. The new baby was translucent pink and appeared to be still in a fluid, transcendent state of radiating white light. We were there, basking in the eye of radiance.

◇

GLOSSARY
OF TERMS USED FREQUENTLY
IN THE TEXT

AKASHIC RECORDS—records of all linear time. To an individual, the records of his or her incarnations on Earth.

ALCHEMY—forcing of the will on matter.

ASTRAL BODY—non-physical body composed of our emotions and auric field which extends out from the physical body.

ASTRAL DIMENSIONS—emotional-body experience existing in simultaneous space with the physical plane.

ASTRAL EMANATIONS—impregnation of consciousness by sounds, images, and suggestions. Television is a powerful source in the present time.

ASTRAL ENERGY—the veil which carries us from lifetime to lifetime, recreating memories in the emotional body in each lifetime.

ASTRAL IMPRINTS—memories of previous experiences contained in the emotional body.

ASTRAL POLLUTION—unwanted energies/entities in the auric field.

ASTRAL SMOKE—radiation of emotions from previous experiences coming from inanimate objects.

ASTRAL STATE—being out of body and existing in the astral dimension.

AURA—electromagnetic field that radiates from the physical body.

AURIC FIELD—vibrating light field around the body which displays the emotional, mental, and physical states.

BLISS—the energy of exhalation after experiencing rapture.

BLUEPRINT—the capsule or repertoire of consciousness that holds us in the third dimension.

BODY—vehicle for truth in the third dimension which echoes spirit.

CELIBACY—abstinence from sexual contact so that energy runs through the body, not outside it.

CELLULAR MEMORY—imprint of emotional-body experiences in the body cells.

CHAKRIC SYSTEM—the seven energy centers of the physical body.

CHILD WITHIN—the being within, which shuts down sometime during childhood and lies within, awaiting reconnection and awakening.

COLORS (as we see them in the auric field)—messages from the emotions created by the length of vibrational frequency. Can be seen by those who can visualize vibration.

COMPASSION—expansion of the emotional body which creates the true merging with others.

CONCEPTION—the moment when the unmanifest takes form; the midpoint, the fission when the egg and sperm unite, which creates universes. The threshold to the unmanifest; the recognition that there is no separation; the center point of the figure eight.

COSMIC JOKE—"You are your higher self!"

COSMIC LAW—"All life moves to perfection!"

CREATION—experiencing and assimilating life, and then reshaping it.

CRIAS—kundalini or electromagnetic energy coursing through the body.

DEATH—a passage, a surrendering into our true self without encumberment.

DEMATERIALIZE—to pass matter from the manifest into the unmanifest.

DIVINE CIRCUITRY—the figure eight, the whole of the body energy which flows through the chakric system and the master glands. The energy itself is sexual energy.

DNA—cellular genetic coding.

ECSTASY—exploding creative force, which carries light when consciousness coalesces itself. The marriage of bliss and rapture. The sourcing, creative force of the universe, the higher self in action.

EGO—the computer which orchestrates the body. The confines of self-limitation which keeps us in the third dimension or reality. It is the structure which allows us to carry out karma.

EMOTIONAL BODY—the emotional vehicle of consciousness which is an entity and vibrates at a low frequency.

ENCRUSTATION—encapsulation of thought forms, prejudices, judgments.

ENLIGHTENMENTS—center of the multidimensional soul; to be able to reach out into the other octaves and pull in our genius capacity.

EXPERIENCING—changing the molecular structure of the body by going through something in a new way, such as past lives, which then translates right-brain perceptions into the third dimension.

FORM—the extension of God in the world; the reach of the divine into matter in order to experience itself.

FUNNEL OF INITIATION—doorway into our inner knowing.

GLOBAL BLUEPRINT—the plan of multitudes of souls to experience something which will wrench the planet through a needed experience.

GRACE—the energetic process of transmutation, transcendence, transformation. It is the process of anchoring the sky, of bringing the soul into Earthly body.

HIGHER SELF—the spiritual vehicle, the power that changes and awakens the emotional body. It is the megaphone of the soul.

HIGHER MIND—the capacity to see the hologram, to perceive the truth in an expanded way. It allows a person to cognate on a higher level, to work on a genius level where both sides of the brain function in synchronicity. It is the genius level itself, the other 90% of the brain.

HOLOGRAM—the overall organizing principle of form, the vision of the higher mind. It is the point when we recognize we are here right now and have also lived many lives.

HOLOGRAPHIC THOUGHT—the left and right brain pulsating in union.

IMPRINT—all the thought forms we have on a soul level, along with all the thought forms of the souls around us whom we have incarnated with.

INCARNATE—to take on the density of physical bodies.

INITIATION—the focusing of intention on the divine and holding it for a long time.

INNER GUIDES—beings which relate to our inner experience at our own level of expertise.

INNER SELF—that part of ourselves which is pushing from within, always trying to get us to spin the hologram of our being to focus on precipitating in those knowings of our Godliness.

INTEGRITY—impermeable encapsulation of self.

JUDGMENT—limitation of consciousness for the protection of the agenda of the emotional body.

KALEIDOSCOPE—a past-life exploration process of going through many lives quickly as you explore a key theme.

KARMA—the responsibilities we can fulfill in a lifetime which will free us from obligations from previous experiences.

KNOWING—living, experiencing, merging, being whole.

LAW OF PERMISSION—the victim and the victimizer are one.

LETTING GO—expanding consciousness so that a person can move out of the constriction of the little self.

LEY LINES—the energy meridians of Earth.

LIGHT BODY—the highest octave of the physical body which exists in the etheric.

LINEARITY—left-brain thought patterns which access only 10% of the brain.

MANIFEST—to take form in the third dimension.

MANIFESTATION—using the harmonics of intention to create what we need.

MASTER GLANDS—the pineal and pituitary glands which radiate huge spans of consciousness from us out into the universe, drawing in energy and information to us. They are our higher-consciousness antennas.

MATERIALIZE—to bring matter into form.

MOTHERING VORTEX—major vortex or energy point where we can more easily quicken our frequency on this planet.

MULTIDIMENSIONALITY—a new brain frequency beyond linearity which allows us to tune into more than one dimension at once.

NADIS—little conglomerates of body energy existing along the fibers spinning out from the chakras within the body, auric field, and nervous system.

NEGATIVE IONS—ions in a negative state which make us feel better. They are especially numerous in mountains, forests, streams, waterfalls, and the ocean.

OCTAVES—the harmonic principle of vibratory resonance in matter. Can be understood by means of the piano keyboard; such as, all the octaves of C vibrate when middle C is struck.

PALPATING—recognizing in an experiential way.

PAST LIVES—previous lifetimes which exist in the emotional body and cellular memory, and can be contacted as a way into the inner resources, the inner points of experience. Working with past lives is a method of contacting multidimensionality in a linear format.

PERCEPTION—the latticework of reality.

PHYSICAL BODY—the organizing vehicle of consciousness which has existence in the third dimension or reality as we know it. It is impregnated with memories and knowledge of its actual matter.

POSITIONALITY—that which orchestrates our perception. What we perceive through the filter of our positionality is our repertoire, which is limited to what we allow in, according to the responses of the emotional body.

PRANA—the divine breath.

PUSHING THE ENVELOPE—recognizing our limits of consciousness and consciously pushing our awareness to higher octaves.

QUICKENING—the expansion of the emotional body out of its positionality so that the higher self can quicken vibration.

RADIANCE—energy resulting from the ecstatic spark, which spreads itself out into the entire spectrum of manifest dimensions and out into the black void of the formless. It pervades all.

RAPTURE—heightened energy of consciousness of the emotional body.

RATIONALITY—the process of funneling information into a place that you think you can control. This promotes separation within our very selves.

REPTILIAN BRAIN—animalistic part of ourselves that warns us of danger, such as radiation or chemical poisoning in the environment.

RESISTANCE—a survival mechanism of the emotional body.

RITUAL—actions taken which are understood in a linear form and which take us into the astral dimension in order to get energy.

SAMADHI—the other end of the tunnel of death, which is ecstatic.

SHAKTI—divine energy which is rejuvenating and empowering.

SEDUCTION—the pull back into the old and familiar ways.

SELF-RIGHTEOUSNESS—a guardian of the emotional body, along with anger and judgment.

SEXUALITY—the inherent quality of our Earth experience which merges us with enlightenment.

SOLAR PLEXUS CHAKRA—the area of our stomach which is the seat of the emotional body.

SOLAR PLEXUS GANGLIA—the sympathetic nervous system of fight or flight, which extends out from the solar plexus.

SPIN POINTS—the images that move us into other dimensions, such as the child within the higher self. We can use them to palpate that which is unseeable, untouchable, imperceptible from our normal human perspective.

SPIRIT—that which is on this side of the veil of manifestation, although it is nonphysical, and holds all the imprints of the emotional body. The energy that interfaces with the material realm.

SPIRITUAL BODY—the most elusive of the four bodies or vehicles of consciousness which comes to us by oscillation, vibrational waves through the grace of the higher self.

STICK-EM—astral energies in the auric field which are emotional memory imprints having weight, matter, and energy. It exists simultaneously with the physical body; it is outside of time and space, and reactivates itself within cellular memory each time we are reborn, until we clear it out.

SURRENDER—that which happens when we finally let go of positionality and just fall back into our real form.

SYNCHRONICITY OF EXPERIENCE—everything is related in some dimension or time.

THIRD DIMENSION—reality as we know and experience it; the manifest plane.

THIRD EYE—the non-physical sight of consciousness.

UNMANIFEST—the created and ever-spiraling enclosed loop of nothingness.

UNSPEAKABLES—actions forbidden in our present reality. Playing through the imprints of past-life emotional experiences allows us to recognize and release our unspeakables.

VEIL—the passage to multidimensionality.

VERTICAL ACCESS—our sexual energy moving through our bodies, moving up through the chakras, which connects us to the source.

VEHICLE—an organizing field which creates action in the physical.

VORTICES—places on Earth which respond to galactic energy.

WINDOWS TO THE SKY—places in consciousness and in the physical body which can bring forth multidimensionality.

WONDERMENT—the state of being filled with wonder when we can embrace our divine selves.

YIN/YANG—the female/male or receptive/projective polarity of consciousness.